Cyrus J. Kephart

Jesus the Nazarene

a brief life of Our Saviour, with a parallel harmony

Cyrus J. Kephart

Jesus the Nazarene
a brief life of Our Saviour, with a parallel harmony

ISBN/EAN: 9783337313777

Printed in Europe, USA, Canada, Australia, Japan

Cover: Foto ©Lupo / pixelio.de

More available books at **www.hansebooks.com**

Jesus the Nazarene

A BRIEF LIFE OF OUR SAVIOUR, WITH

A PARALLEL HARMONY

BY

REV. C. J. KEPHART, A.M.

AUTHOR OF "THE PUBLIC LIFE OF CHRIST," AND
"LIFE OF JESUS FOR CHILDREN"

WITH INTRODUCTION BY
REV. C. R. BLACKALL

DAYTON, OHIO
W. J. SHUEY, PUBLISHER
1894

TO

Father and Mother,

WHO FOR MANY YEARS WALKED HAND IN HAND

WITH

THE LIVING CHRIST

AND

WHOSE LIVES WERE AN INSPIRATION AND A BENEDICTION

TO ALL WHO KNEW THEM, THESE PAGES

ARE DEDICATED BY

The Author.

INTRODUCTION.

IF there were any need of evidence to prove the all-pervasiveness of the Name that is above every other name, and the power which that Name exercises the whole world over, it would be found in the continually increasing number of volumes that appear with Jesus Christ the Nazarene, Son of man and Son of God, as their subject. This latest contribution to the literature of a theme worthy of the angels' songs is timely, in view of the fact that in all lands where the International Lessons are used the God-man will be studied, in a course extending through an entire year, his life and work being presented in chronological order.

The name of Jesus Christ appears but little in contemporaneous history; hence we are limited as to sources of information. If the Gospels had been written in such order and completeness that a perfect biography could be constructed, the way would be clear; but they are manifestly very far from being full along certain directions knowledge in regard to which would give satisfaction to the careful inquirer. If they had been written each to supplement the others, there would still be a clear path and the possibility of definite agreement upon certain questions of fact concerning which there is divergence.

The advantages of having four distinct and independent narratives of our Lord's work and teachings while in this world, however, are entirely evident. No one felt called to write a detailed life of the Master until the original sources of information had passed away forever. There can be no contention, then, as to authority in the matter, and we are shut up to a comparison of the four Gospels to ascertain and arrange the facts as best we may. Under the circumstances it is not remarkable that questions should arise upon which wise men should differ, and hence criticism should result upon the best work that can be done; but fortunately these differences are not in any instance vital to the facts themselves, but only as to the sequence of the facts, while each writer, being fully convinced of the accuracy of his own investigations, may necessarily seem more or less dogmatic in statement. The study given by the author in the preparation of his excellent work, "The Public Life of Christ," fitted him well to tell this story of the life and work and teachings of Jesus the Christ; in fact, the one supplements the other so thoroughly that they will no doubt be used much together.

The arrangement whereby reference can at a glance be made to the several Gospels that state given facts will materially aid the general reader and the student, while the use of the Revised Version for quotations is an obvious advantage. The author has been wise in not cumbering his text with descriptions of persons and places, and thus interfering with the easy flow of the story; the appendix, however, supplies answers to queries sufficient for the time, until a Bible dictionary can be consulted for fuller details. The volume has been prepared with reference to the practical needs of busy people; hence the story is in outline, as a hand-book, but it will stimulate thought and engender an earnest desire to delve yet deeper in the Gospel mine for the rich gems that may be gained by any one who will honestly seek; for in no regard is it more true than in this, that they who seek will surely find.

C. R. BLACKALL.

Philadelphia, May, 1894.

CONTENTS.

V

CHAPTER V.

THE THIRD PUBLIC YEAR. A.D. 29.

CHAPTER VI.

THREE MONTHS IN SECLUSION. A.D. 30.

CHAPTER VII.

PASSION WEEK.

CHAPTER VIII.

RESURRECTION, APPEARANCES, AND ASCENSION.

APPENDIX.

AUTHORITIES.

In presenting this book to the public, I desire to state that in its preparation I was materially assisted by the following works: Andrews' "Life of Our Lord," Alford's "Greek Testament," Farrar's "Life of Christ," Edersheim's "The Life and Times of Jesus the Messiah," Geikie's "Life and Words of Christ," McClintock and Strong's "Encyclopœdia," Thomson's "The Land and the Book," and Hurlbut's "Manual of Biblical Geography."

In all quotations from Scripture the Revised Version is used.

C. J. K.

JESUS THE NAZARENE.

CHAPTER I.

CHRONOLOGY OF THE GOSPEL PERIOD.

I. *When Was Jesus Born?*

THE Gospels do not give the date. Only Matthew and Luke give any record of his birth. Matthew says (2 : 1) that it occurred "in the days of Herod the king." But as Herod ruled at least thirty-eight years, this statement does not assist us to a definite date. Luke tells us (2 : 1-7) that Jesus was born while Joseph and Mary were at Bethlehem to be enrolled, in obedience to the decree of Augustus Cæsar. But Augustus ordered three separate censuses of the empire to be taken, one in the year of Rome 726, one in 746, and one in 767. Which of these is the one referred to by Luke? The first is evidently too early, and the last just as evidently too late. Hence, we conclude that the census ordered by Augustus in 746 is the one referred to in Luke's Gospel. But as it required several years to complete the enrollment of the citizens of the empire, we do not from this datum reach a conclusion as to the year of the birth. We do, however, reach a date *before* which the birth of Jesus did not occur. That is, Jesus was not born earlier than A.U.C. 746, B.C. 8.

Can we reach a date after which his birth did not occur? Matthew tells us (2 : 15, 19) that the death of Herod occurred after the birth of Jesus. From statements made by Josephus, it is estimated that Herod died between March 13 and April 4, A.U.C. 750, B.C. 4,[1] Jesus being yet a child. This, then, gives a date *after* which Jesus was

---

[1] See Andrews, p. 1.

not born. These data fix the period within which the birth of Jesus occurred; that is, between the Roman years 746 and 750. Beyond this, certainty cannot be reached. Data that will appear in the discussion of the second question in this chapter point to A.U.C. 749 as the year; that is, B.C. 5.

As to the time of the year, we may get some help from Luke. He tells us (1 : 5-14) that the birth of John the Baptist was announced to Zacharias, a priest of the course of Abia, while he was in the discharge of his duties in the temple. The birth of John preceded the birth of Jesus by about six months (Luke 1 : 36). If the birth of Jesus occurred in 749, this announcement must have been made to Zacharias not later than some time in 748. From Talmudical state-ments and from statements in Josephus, it is estimated that the course of Abia served in the temple, in the year 748, during the week April 17-23, and again in October, 3-9.[1] During one of these periods, therefore, we conclude that Zacharias received the promise of the birth of John. This puts the birth of Jesus, which occurred fifteen months after the annunciation to Zacharias, either near the middle of A.U.C. 749, or in December of 749, or in January of 750. Tradition favors December, and there are no strong arguments against it.

II. *When Was Jesus Baptized?*

The Gospels give no specific reply. Matthew and Mark simply state (Matt. 3; Mark 1 : 1-10) that he was baptized during the min-istry of John the Baptist. John gives no account of the baptism of Jesus. Luke says (3 : 1, 2) that "the word of God came unto John" "in the fifteenth year of the reign of Tiberius Cæsar." This marks the beginning of the ministry of John the Baptist as occurring in the fifteenth year of Tiberius's reign. John had probably been preaching some months when Jesus came to him for baptism. At the time of his baptism Jesus "began to be about thirty years of age" (Luke 3 : 23).

When was the fifteenth year of Tiberius's reign? He became

[1] Andrews, p. 13.

associate ruler with his step-father, Augustus, in the year of Rome 764, and three years later became sole ruler. If in estimating his fifteenth year we count from 767, the year in which he became sole ruler, we shall reach 782 as his fifteenth year. Subtracting from this thirty years, the age of Jesus at his baptism, we have 752 as the year of his birth. But we have seen above that the death of Herod, which occurred after the birth of Jesus, is not to be placed later than 750; hence, 752 cannot be, according to this estimate, the year of Jesus' birth, nor can 782 be the fifteenth year of Tiberius. But if in estimating the fifteenth year of Tiberius we count from the beginning of his associate reign, 764, then we reach 779 as his fifteenth year, and 749 as the year of the birth of Jesus, a date in full accord with all ascertained data. We therefore take 779 as the fifteenth year of Tiberius. John began baptizing at some time in this year; we do not know at just what time, probably during the summer shortly after having reached the age of thirty. We hence conclude that Jesus was baptized in the latter part of 779 or the beginning of 780, A.D. 26 or 27. Tradition gives January 6 as the day of the month.

III. *When Was Jesus Crucified?*

The crucifixion occurred during the feast of the Passover, which came annually in the month of Nisan, corresponding with the moon of our March or April. This, however, determines neither the year, nor the day of the month, nor the day of the week.

Friday is very generally accepted as the day of the week, although some have argued for Thursday; their premises, however, are very unsatisfactory.

The decision as to the day of the month depends upon the answer to another inquiry: Did the crucifixion occur before or after the eating of the Passover supper? John 13 : 1, in connection with what follows, seems to indicate that the supper there spoken of was eaten before the Passover; verse 29 speaks as though some preparation for the Passover yet remained to be made; John 18 : 28, referring to a time after Jesus and the disciples had eaten, seems to say that

the Passover had not yet been eaten; John in 19:14, 31 speaks of
the day of the crucifixion as "the Preparation of the passover."
These statements taken by themselves would no doubt lead to the
conclusion that the crucifixion occurred before the Passover supper.
Turning to the other Gospels, we find statements quite different.
Matthew 26:17-21, Mark 14:12-18, Luke 22:7-15, all state with great
clearness that the Passover was eaten by Jesus with his disciples, and
hence, that it occurred before the crucifixion.

It is not to be denied that there is in the Gospels a difference in
statement upon this point; but that there is a contradiction in their
statements does not follow. Different explanations have been given.
Probably if we understood fully the use of terms by each of the
Evangelists, we should have no difficulty in seeing that they agree,
and that Jesus did eat the Passover before the crucifixion. The
following suggestions may help to the solution of the difficulty:
(1) The statement of John 13:1 does not necessarily denote a time
in immediate chronological connection with the supper spoken of in
the remainder of the chapter. (2) Verse 29 may mean that the
disciples thought that Judas went out to get something for the
remaining days of the feast, as the feasting continued during seven
days. (3) The words, "the passover," of 18:28, may be used by
John in a general sense to designate the feast of the entire week,
and not technically of the Passover supper. (4) The expression
of John 19:14, 31, "the Preparation of the passover," may mean
the preparation day of the Passover week; that is, the day of the
preparation for Sabbath of Passover week.[1]

If Jesus did eat the Passover supper with his disciples, as the
writer accepts, then the crucifixion occurred on 15th Nisan, because
the Passover supper was always eaten on the evening of 14th Nisan
after the slaying of the lamb on the afternoon of the same day.

But this does not fix the *year* of the crucifixion. It is held that
astronomical calculations show that between the years A.D. 25 and
35 only the years 27, 30, and 33 had 14th Nisan on Thursday. This

[1] Andrews, pp. 465-481.

argues strongly for the year 30 as the year of the crucifixion, since 27 is too early and 33 too late. But as the calendar was not so carefully kept then as now, this cannot be relied upon with certainty.

Are we assisted by Scripture statements relative to the length of Jesus' ministry?

The Gospels do not give us any definite statement as to the length of time spent by Jesus in his public work. This has led to comparative research that has resulted in conclusions widely diverse. Neither Matthew, nor Mark, nor Luke gives any indications as to the length of Jesus' ministry. They do not mention his presence in Judæa after his departure following the imprisonment of John the Baptist (Matt. 4:12; Mark 1:14; Luke 4:14) until his return to the crucifixion (Matt. 20:17; Mark 10:32; Luke 18:31); nor do they give any indication as to the length of time intervening between his baptism and the arrest of John. They make no reference to any feast during his ministry except the Passover at the close of his life. John gives quite a different record, and yet he does not clearly answer our inquiry. He says nothing of the baptism or temptation of Jesus, but speaks of events intimately connected therewith. He records two journeys from Judæa to Galilee (John 1:43 and 4:3), with a third clearly implied (compare John 5 with 6:1). He also names three journeys to Jerusalem, not including the journey to his baptism (John 2:13; 5:1; 7:10). These all seem to have been from Galilee. He also speaks of six feasts that occurred during his public life: three Passovers (John 2:13; 6:4; 12:1 and following); one feast of Tabernacles (John 7); one feast of Dedication (John 10:22); and one feast the name of which he does not give (John 5:1).

If from any of these data we are to gain help in deciding the length of our Lord's ministry, it must be from the statements respecting the Passover, as this is the only feast repeated; the others might all have occurred within one year. If we can decide definitely the number of Passovers during his ministry, we can

decide the length of the ministry, as the Passover occurred annually.
If there were three Passovers, his public life must have covered at
least two years and a few months, since he was baptized some-
time before the first Passover named during his public life (John
1 : 26-33; 2 : 13). Although three Passovers are named by John, some
hold that there were only two, explaining the words, "the passover," of John 6 : 4, as a gloss, and holding that the feast there
named was identical with the feast of Tabernacles mentioned in
John 7. This would reduce his ministry to one year and a few
months, as some hold. But the theory is untenable, and now
generally abandoned.

But were there only three Passovers?

The answer to this depends largely upon our interpretation of
John 5 : 1. What feast was this "feast of the Jews," the name of
which John does not give? They had a number of feasts—Purim,
in March; Passover, in March-April; Pentecost, in May; Tabernacles,
in October; Dedication, in December; Trumpets, which occurred
monthly; and Wood-gathering, which occurred several times in the
year. If nothing else were necessary to meet the conditions than
that the gathering be a feast, then any one of these might be the
one referred to in John 5 : 1. If the one there named was any one
except a Passover, then it would be possible to give an arrangement
which would put all the events of the Saviour's public life within
two years and a fraction. If it was a Passover, then three years
and a fraction are necessary, as this will give four Passovers.

Can we decide what feast this was?

It evidently occurred between the Passover of John 2 : 13 and that
named in John 6 : 4. Between these feasts occurred also the Judæan
ministry of Jesus (John 3 : 22). It is very generally held that this
ministry occupied several months; that is, that it began very soon
after the Passover of A.D. 27, and continued till about November
or December of the same year. If this be correct, then the feast
of 5 : 1 could not have been either Pentecost or Tabernacles of
that year, as Jesus very evidently "went up" to this feast from

Galilee after the Judæan ministry had closed. There have been no advocates for Dedication, and very few for either of the minor feasts, as they were gatherings of little significance. This would render it probable that the feast of John 5 : 1 was either Purim or Passover of A.D. 28. A number of able writers have held for Purim,[1] most of whom estimate the length of Jesus' ministry at two years and a fraction. This was, however, also a feast of minor importance, having originated in Persia, not by divine appointment, but in commemoration of the preservation of the Jews from the plots of Haman; it is not certain that this feast was largely attended by the Jews. Other writers of equal eminence prefer Passover,[2] as it was the great feast of the Jewish nation, and was more largely attended than any of the others. Accepting Passover, we have three years and three months as the length of time occupied by our Lord in his ministry, a period more in harmony with the work done by him than one either shorter or longer. This also brings the crucifixion in the year 30, in harmony with conclusions already reached.

What was the hour of the crucifixion?

Mark says (15 : 25), "And it was the third hour, and they crucified him." John says (19 : 14), referring to the close of the trial of Jesus, "It was . . . . about the sixth hour." This difference of statement has given rise to much discussion, and to various explanations, none of which are entirely satisfactory. The time given by Mark—the third hour, about 9 A.M —most fully harmonizes with all the narrated circumstances.

Restating conclusions, we have the following dates quite satisfactorily determined:—

Jesus was born December, A.U.C. 749, B.C. 5.

He was baptized either late A.U.C. 779, A.D. 26, or early A.U.C. 780, A.D. 27.

The crucifixion occurred 9 A.M., Nisan 15, April 7, A.U.C. 783, A.D. 30.

---

[1] Tischendorf, Meyer, Wieseler, Farrar, Weiss, and others.

[2] Lightfoot, Grotius, Greswell, Wordsworth, Weitbrecht, Andrews, and others.

IV. *Contemporaneous Events.*

Palestine became subject to Rome B.C. 63, and so remained until the dissolution of the empire. Augustus Cæsar reigned B.C. 30 to A.D. 14. Tiberius Cæsar succeeded him, and reigned A.D. 14 to A.D. 37.

Herod the Great was made king of all Palestine B.C. 40, and reigned until his death, A.D. 4. At his death his kingdom was divided among his three sons. Archelaus received Judæa and Samaria, with the title of ethnarch, and ruled until A.D. 6, when he was banished to Vienna, in Gaul. Herod Antipas received Galilee and Peræa, with the title of tetrarch, and ruled until A.D. 38, when he was banished to Lyons, in Gaul; later he removed to Spain, where he died. Herod Philip received the Bashan district, all east of the Jordan except Peræa, with the title of tetrarch, and ruled until his death, in A.D. 34.

After the banishment of Archelaus, Judæa and Samaria were annexed directly to the empire, as part of the province of Syria, and were governed by the following procurators: Coponius, A.D. 6-9; Marcus Ambivius, A.D. 9-12; Annius Rufus, A.D. 12-15; Valerius Gratus, A.D. 15-26; Pontius Pilate, A.D. 26-36, with others following down to the destruction of the city, A.D. 70.

These data furnish us the following facts relative to the life of Jesus: First, his birth occurred while Augustus Cæsar was emperor of Rome; second, from the early childhood of Jesus until after his death Herod Antipas ruled in Galilee and Peræa, and during the same period Herod Philip ruled in the Bashan district, while Judæa and Samaria were ruled by a succession of procurators; third, the public life of Jesus occurred while Tiberius Cæsar was emperor of Rome and Pontius Pilate was procurator of Judæa and Samaria.

The inhabitants of Judæa in New Testament times were largely descendants of Hebrews returned from the Babylonian captivity. The inhabitants of Samaria were descendants of Cuthite and other Assyrian colonists imported after the Assyrian captivity. (See II. Kings 17, and Trench on the Parable of the Good Samaritan.) Galilee was occupied chiefly by Jews less superstitious than those of Judæa. Peræa and the Bashan district were occupied by Jews and Gentiles, who intermingled but little.

The great majority of the people were abjectly poor, and because of their inability to observe the law with the exactness required by the interpretation of the Rabbis, were virtually outcasts in the eyes of the religionists of the times.

The temple of New Testament times was begun by Herod B.C. 20-17, but was not completed until A.D. 65. Here the devout Jews of all Palestine, and indeed of all the world, assembled statedly for worship. The Samaritans worshiped at Mt. Gerizim, where was a temple built by Sanballat, with the consent of Alexander the Great, about B.C. 325.

2

THE INTRODUCTORY PERIOD. B.C. 6 TO A.D. 26.

Matt.	Mark.		Luke.	John.

In October of the year of Rome 748, B.C. 6, while Zacharias was in the discharge of his priestly duties at Jerusalem, an angel of the Lord appeared to him and announced that his wife Elizabeth, hitherto childless, should bear a son who should be named John; that he should "go before his [the Lord's] face in the spirit and power of Elijah" (Luke). Delighted, yet doubting, Zacharias returned to his home in the hill country of Judæa, probably Hebron, where the child was born in June of B.C. 5. "And the child grew, and waxed strong in spirit, and was in the deserts till the day of his showing unto Israel" (Luke 1:80).

Luke. 1:5

Six months after the annunciation to Zacharias, the angel Gabriel came to Mary, a virgin of Nazareth in Galilee, a descendant of David, the espoused of Joseph a carpenter, and promised to her the miraculous conception of a son, whom she should name Jesus, saying, "He shall be great, and shall be called the Son of the Most High: and the Lord God shall give unto him the throne of his father David: and he shall reign over the house of Jacob for ever; and of his kingdom there shall be no end" (Luke).

to

1:38.

[1] NOTE.—In the following pages, marginal references are employed to indicate the Scripture passages relating to the various incidents in the life of Jesus. A reference placed under a horizontal line indicates the beginning, and one placed above a horizontal line indicates the end, of that portion of the narrative to which the Scripture reference applies.

Matt.	Mark.		Luke.	John.
1:19 to 1:25.			2:1 to	

Some time after this the angel of the Lord appeared to Joseph in a dream, and informed him of God's purpose in relation to his espoused wife, and directed him also to call the name of the child "Jesus; for it is he that shall save his people from their sins" (Matthew).

About this same time Augustus Cæsar ordered that a census of the empire should be taken. In answer to this requirement, and according to Jewish custom, Joseph and Mary, now husband and wife, went to the village of Bethlehem in Judæa, the city of David, to be registered. Many others having come on a like errand, Bethlehem was over-crowded, so that Joseph and Mary found it necessary to take shelter in a cave.[1] Shortly afterward Mary gave birth to her firstborn, Jesus the Son of man, the Son of God.

Thus quietly and in great humility occurred the birth of the world's Redeemer. But the birth of Jesus, unnoticed by men, was not wholly unheralded. To a company of shepherds keeping watch over their flocks near Bethlehem, the angel of the Lord appeared with the message, "Be not afraid; for behold, I bring you good tidings of great joy which shall be to all the people: for there is born to

[1] "The sacred spot where Jesus was born is pointed out as in a cave under the high altar of the great Church of the Nativity. Nor is there anything improbable in a cave being thus honored, for it is quite common in Palestine to build a house against the mouth of such a natural chamber, to have the benefit of it either as a stable or a lumber-room. You go down by a flight of steps to the supposed 'stable,' now made into a kind of room by hangings, once splendid, on the walls and roof. Two huge gilt candlesticks rise in the corner; a wall altar, over which is a smoke-blackened picture, takes up some space, and below, rising from the ground at the same side, is a small scallop-shaped recess, fringed with lamps always burning, and paved with various colored marble, forming a star with a silver center, while along the outer edge there run the words, in Latin, 'Here Jesus Christ was born of the Virgin Mary.' I frankly confess that the spot had a mighty power over me, for it has really very high claims to be regarded as genuine, tradition having marked it as such since the second century."—*Geikie's "New Testament Hours," pp. 4, 5.*

Matt.	Mark.		Luke.	John.

you this day in the city of David a Saviour, which is Christ the Lord." And suddenly a multitude of the heavenly host took up the refrain,—

"Glory to God in the highest,
And on earth peace among men in whom he is well pleased " (Luke).

On the eighth day the child was circumcised and named Jesus. At the end of forty days he was presented in the temple, where he was met and greeted by the aged and devout Simeon and by the prophetess Anna. *(2:39.)*

2:1

Shortly after this occurred the visit of the Magi, who, directed of God, came "from the east to . . . Jerusalem," and asked: "Where is he that is born King of the Jews? for we saw his star in the east, and are come to worship him" (Matthew). This inquiry aroused the ever jealous Herod, and he immediately set about seeking "the young child to destroy him" (Matthew). Warned of God, Joseph and Mary fled with the child to Egypt for refuge, and remained there until after the death of Herod.[1] Learning that the Magi did not return as he requested, Herod ordered the slaughter of all the children of Bethlehem from two years old and under—an awful picture of the heart of this vicious king.

to

At length, informed of the death of Herod, the Holy Family returned to Palestine. Avoiding Judæa for fear of Archelaus, they went directly to Nazareth in Galilee.

2:23

Of the further events of the childhood and early manhood of Jesus we know but *(2:39)*

---

[1] The flight into Egypt must have occurred not later than the early part of B.C. 4, for Herod died only a few days before the Passover of that year. How long before his death their flight occurred we do not know, and hence cannot determine the length of time they remained in Egypt. Scholars are divided in their estimate between a few months and as many years.

Matt.	*Mark.*		*Luke.*	*John.*
		little. At the age of twelve he was taken to the feast of the Passover at Jerusalem for the first time. The story of his being missed by his parents and of their finding him in the temple in the midst of the doctors of the law, is one of too great beauty to be told in language other than that of Holy Writ. Read it in Luke 2 : 42-49.	*to* *2:50.*	

Of the events of the Saviour's life between this visit to the Passover and his entrance upon his public ministry, we only know that "he went down with them [his parents], and came to Nazareth; and he was subject unto them," and "advanced in wisdom and stature, and in favour with God and men" (Luke 2 : 51, 52).

He learned the carpenter's trade (Mark 6 : 3), and, as Justin Martyr writes, "did make, while among men, ploughs and yokes, thus setting before them symbols of righteousness, and teaching them an active life."

From the fact that the records of his later life contain no reference to Joseph, his reputed father, it is thought that Joseph died before Jesus began his public ministry.

The Gospels maintain even a more complete silence respecting the childhood, youth, and early manhood of John the Baptist. Aside from the statement of Luke 1 : 80, we know nothing of his life from the day of his circumcision until he appeared in the wilderness of Judæa with the same abruptness that characterized the first appearance of his great ancestor, the prophet Elijah.

CHAPTER III.

The First Public Year. a.d. 27.

Matt.	Mark.	January-February.	Luke.	John.
3:1	1:1	"In those days cometh John the Baptist, preaching in the wilderness of Judæa" (Matthew). He had been preaching some time—it may be, several months—when Jesus came for baptism. His work was very successful, so that multitudes from "Jerusalem, and all Judæa, and all the region round about Jordan" came to him, "and they were baptized of him in the river Jordan, confessing their sins" (Matthew).	3:1	
to	to	At length Jesus came from Nazareth in Galilee to be baptized. John at first hesitated, but at length consented, and baptized him. As Jesus came up out of the water, the Holy Spirit came upon him in the form of a dove, and God the Father testified in an audible voice that Jesus was his beloved Son.	to	
4:11.	1:14.	Immediately Jesus was led of the Spirit into the wilderness "to be tempted of the devil." Here the Saviour spent forty days and forty nights in fasting, at the close of which he hungered. In the course of his temptation he was taken to a pinnacle of the temple, and also to an exceeding high mountain. At the close of the temptation "angels came and ministered unto him" (Matthew).	4:13.	
		During the temptation of Jesus, John		1:19

22

Matt.	*Mark.*		*Luke.*	*John.*

the Baptist remained at Bethabara, teaching and baptizing. Meanwhile a deputation of Levites came to him from Jerusalem and asked him whether he was the Messiah. John replied with a distinct denial. On the next day Jesus returned from the temptation, and as he approached, John pointed him out as the Messiah, in the language, "Behold, the Lamb of God, which taketh away the sin of the world!" (John.) The next day he repeated the announcement, and two of his disciples, Andrew and John, left John and became disciples of Jesus. Andrew shortly afterward found his brother Simon and brought him to Jesus, who at once named him Cephas, a stone. Accompanied by these his first followers, Jesus started to Galilee, and on the way secured two more disciples, Philip and Nathanael. Three days later he arrived at Cana, where with his mother and newly secured disciples he attended a wedding. Here he performed his first miracle, turning six water-pots of water into wine.

to

March.

After the wedding, Jesus, with his mother, brethren, and disciples, made a short visit to Capernaum.[1]

2:12.

April-November.

After a short stay at Capernaum Jesus went up to Jerusalem to the Passover.[2] During the feast he cleansed the temple, driving out those who were polluting it by using it for mercenary purposes. Here

2:13

[1] Of what occurred during this visit we are not informed.
[2] The Passover occurred this year April 11-17. (Andrews, p. 169.)

Matt.	Mark.		Luke.	John.

he also gave his first recorded public teaching. The Jews were at once aroused to opposition because of his claiming such unusual authority, and their demands rendered necessary his first personal vindication. During the feast he wrought a number of miracles, in consequence of which many believed. He was visited privately by Nicodemus, a ruler of the Jews, a member of the Sanhedrin, to whom he spoke with great force of the necessity and nature of the "new birth." After the feast, taking his disciples, the number of whom had increased somewhat, he withdrew to the country, where he engaged for some time in teaching and baptizing, John the Baptist being similarly engaged at Ænon.[1]

John.

to

3:23.

December.

"When therefore the Lord knew how that the Pharisees had heard that Jesus was making and baptizing more disciples than John, ... he left Judæa, and departed again into Galilee" (John). At this point Jesus practically closed his Judæan ministry; his visits to this region after this were only of short duration, and were not especially for teaching.

In going to Galilee he went through Samaria, passing Jacob's well near Sychar. Here occurred the conversation with the woman of Samaria, in the course of which Jesus gave his first announcement of his Messiahship. He tarried in the city two days, and taught, in response

4:1

---

[1] What parts of Judæa were visited by Jesus during this time we are not told, nor are we told the length of time thus occupied by him. It is probable, and generally believed, that it covered some months, perhaps April to November inclusive; that is, almost the whole of our Lord's first public year seems to have been spent in Judæa. "Jesus himself baptized not, but his disciples" (John 4:2).

Matt	Mark.		Luke.	John.

to which many believed. Leaving Samaria, he went to Galilee, where he was received with expressions of great esteem, many of the Galileans having been present and witnessed what he did at the feast at Jerusalem.

to

He came at length to Cana, where he was visited by a nobleman from Capernaum, who requested that he would "come down, and heal his son," who was lying at Capernaum "at the point of death" (John). Without going to Capernaum Jesus granted his request by healing his son, though he was seventeen miles distant. This was the second miracle that he performed at Cana. From all that we can learn we conclude that Jesus now spent some months in retirement, taking rest. His disciples meanwhile returned to their own homes and to their business, fishing. During this interval the first year of our Lord's public life closed.

4:54.

CHAPTER IV.

THE SECOND PUBLIC YEAR. A.D. 28.

Matt.	Mark.	*January-April.*	Luke.	John.
				5:1

AFTER spending some time in retirement Jesus went again to Jerusalem to the Passover,[1] "a feast of the Jews." While at the feast he healed an impotent man at the pool of Bethesda on the Sabbath day. This aroused great opposition upon the part of the Jews, extending even to a conspiracy to take his life. Notwithstanding this opposition, Jesus continued to teach, speaking very plainly of his relation to the Father, of his own work, and of the conditions necessary to personal salvation.

(John: to)

(John: 5:17.)

(Matt. 4:12. Mark 1:14, 15.) Learning about this time that John the Baptist had been arrested and thrown into prison, Jesus withdrew again to Galilee, and on his way passed through Nazareth. On the Sabbath he went into the synagogue, and being accorded the privilege of speaking, he read from Isaiah 61 : 1, 2, and preached. The people were at first greatly delighted "at the words of grace which proceeded out of his mouth" (Luke), but at length became offended, and attempted to cast him headlong over the brow of the hill on which the city was *(Matt. 4:13)* built. Passing through their midst, he went again to Capernaum. He now se-

(Luke: 4:11 to 4:31.)

---

[1] Date of feast, March 30-April 5. (Andrews, p. 189.)

Matt.	Mark.		Luke.	John
to	1:16-20	lected this as his home, and entered fully upon his ministry in Galilee.	5:1	
4:22.		He proceeded first to re-collect his disciples, who, some months before, had returned to their homes.[1] In connection with this second call occurred the first miraculous draught of fishes, which so excited Peter that he "fell down at Jesus' knees, saying, Depart from me; for I am a sinful man, O Lord." Jesus replied, "Fear not; from henceforth thou shalt catch men" (Luke). After this, Jesus went into the synagogues on the Sabbath	to	
			5:11.	
	1:21	days and taught. On the first Sabbath there was a demoniac present in the synagogue, and Jesus, with a word, healed	4:32	
8:14-17.		him, to the amazement of all. Afterward he retired to the home of Peter, where he healed Peter's mother-in-law, and after sunset of the same day he healed multitudes who were suffering from various afflictions.	to	
			4:41	

May-August.

Matt.	Mark.		Luke.	John
	to	The next morning, rising very early, he went out to a place of seclusion to	5:16.	
4:23-25.		pray. Peter found him at length, and urged him to return to Capernaum, as the multitudes were waiting to hear him. But he replied, "I must preach the good tidings of the kingdom of God to the other cities also" (Luke), and he started		
8:2-4. (?)		on his first circuit through the towns and villages about Capernaum. During this	4:42-44.	
	1:45.	circuit he taught and healed many.	5:12-15. (?)	
9:2	2:1	At length he returned to Capernaum, where great multitudes gathered at once to hear him. Many sick were brought for healing, among them a paralytic,	5:17	

[1] See page 25.

Matt.	Mark.		Luke.	John.
		who, because of the multitude present, was let down into his presence through the roof. All were healed. These things, while they excited the common people greatly in his favor, only served to arouse the enmity of the Pharisees, and when		
to	*to*	he announced the forgiveness of the sins of the paralytic, they openly charged him with blasphemy. At length he withdrew to the seashore, where he saw Levi, a publican, collecting tribute. Upon Jesus' requesting him to become one of his disciples, Levi gave up his business	*to*	
9:9.	2:14	and followed him.[1]	5:28.·	
12:1	2:23	After the call of Levi, Jesus and his disciples, while journeying in and about Capernaum, on a certain Sabbath passed through a field of wheat or barley. As they passed along, the disciples plucked a few heads of grain and rubbed them in their hands to get the kernels. The Pharisees, seeing this, and noticing also that Jesus did not reprove the disciples, became greatly incensed, because, as they claimed, he was tolerating the violation of the law of the Sabbath. But Jesus vin-	6:1	
to	*to*	dicated the disciples, and in a word taught the Pharisees and the world the true doctrine of the Sabbath. "The Sabbath," said he, "was made for man, and not man for the Sabbath" (Mark). On a Sabbath following he went into the synagogue in Capernaum and taught. There was a man present with a withered hand, and the Pharisees watched anxiously to see whether he would heal him on the Sab-	*to*	

[1] Some authors place the feast given to Jesus by Levi immediately after Jesus called him. But as Matthew puts Levi's feast immediately preceding the raising of Jairus's daughter, and connects the two very closely, and as Mark and Luke both place that miracle after Jesus' return from Gadara, which, according to all three of the Synoptists, occurred some considerable time after the call of Levi, the author prefers to place Levi's feast not in immediate connection with his call, but at a later date. See page 32.

Matt.	Mark.		Luke.	John.
		bath day. He did so, and they withdrew in anger, and with the Herodians, with whom they had been at enmity, conspired for his destruction. Jesus withdrew again to the seashore, where he addressed the multitudes from a small vessel, accompanying his teaching with numerous and	6:11.	
12:21.	3:12.	various works of healing.		
	3:13-19.	After this he withdrew to a mountain, evidently not far from Capernaum, where he spent the night in prayer.[1] The next morning he chose the twelve apostles, and upon the assembling of a great multitude	6:12	
Chs.5-7.		of people he delivered the Sermon on the	to	
8:5-13.		Mount. After this he returned again to Capernaum, where occurred, probably on the day of his return, the healing of the		
		centurion's servant. The crowds around him became so great, and the demands upon him so numerous, that he could	7:10.	
	3:20, 21.	not find time to eat. Learning this, his friends sought to get him away from the people, saying, "He is beside himself" (Mark).		
		Shortly after this, accompanied by his disciples and a number of others, Jesus started on his second circuit through Galilee, and on the way came to the city of Nain. As they approached the gate of the city they met a funeral procession bearing to burial the only son of a widow. Jesus touched the bier and bade the young man "Arise," and he was delivered to his mother alive. This is the first recorded raising of the dead by our Lord.	7:11	

September-December.

11:1		John the Baptist, who had been now for several months a prisoner in the fort-		

[1] Probably the Horns of Hattin, west of the Sea of Galilee. Some authors prefer Mt. Tabor.

Matt. | *Mark.* | ... | *Luke.* | *John.*

ress of Machærus, in the southern part of Peræa, hearing of the wonderful works of Jesus,—surprised, it may be, that one so mighty should leave his forerunner in such distress,—sent two of his disciples to ask Jesus, "Art thou he that cometh or look we for another?" (Luke.) They found Jesus some time after the miracle at Nain, probably yet in that vicinity, and propounded to him the question given them by John. Instead of answering directly, Jesus cited his words and works in proof of his person and character. After their departure Jesus pronounced a most glowing compliment upon the character and work of John the Baptist, but added the significant remark, "He that is least in the kingdom of God is greater than he." Following this, he began "to upbraid the cities wherein most of his mighty works were done, because they repented not" (Matthew).

Closely related to these events, probably both as to time and place, occurred another most interesting incident. Jesus was invited by one Simon, a Pharisee, to dine with him. While at the table eating, a woman with an unenviable reputation came in, and standing behind the Saviour, washed his feet with her tears and wiped them with her loosely flowing hair, and following this, kissed his feet and anointed him. The fact that Jesus allowed a woman of such character to take such liberties, offended the Pharisee. Jesus, knowing his feelings, spoke to him the parable of the Two Debtors, in which he most positively, yet most beautifully and tenderly, revealed to the Pharisee and to the world his hatred of hypocrisy and his unconquerable love for penitent sin-

Luke column: *to* ... 7:35. — 7:36 ... *to*

Matt column: *to* ... 11:50

John column: (blank)

Matt.	Mark.		Luke.	John.
		ners. Then turning to the woman, he said, "Thy faith hath saved thee; go in peace" (Matthew).		
		Following this, he continued his travels through Galilee, "preaching and bringing the good tidings of the kingdom of God" (Luke), being accompanied by the Twelve, a number of devout women, and many others.	8:3.	
12:22	3:22	At length he returned to Capernaum, where was brought to him one possessed of a devil, blind and dumb. Jesus at once healed him, greatly to the amazement of all. Certain scribes from Jerusalem, upon hearing of the miracle, became enraged, and charged him with being in league with Beelzebub, the prince of the devils, a charge repeated a number of times afterward. Jesus rebuked them in very plain and forcible language, and to their request for a sign, referred them		
to	to	to the sign of the prophet Jonas. While he was speaking, his mother and his brethren sought for him, and to the multitude he announced that his true kindred are those who do the will of God. On the same day he went out by the seaside, and when the multitudes came together he entered a boat and taught them, uttering the first group of parables recorded: the Sower, the Tares, the Mustard Seed, the Leaven, the Hid Treasure, the Goodly Pearl, and the Draw-net. They may or they may not all have been spoken on one day. Some of them seem to have	8:19-21. 8:4 to 8:18.	
13:52.	4:34.	been spoken to the disciples only.		
8:18.		Toward evening Jesus proposed to cross to the other side of the sea, and while they were preparing to do so, he held a conversation with a certain scribe and one of his disciples concerning "follow-	9:57-60.	

Matt.	Mark		Luke.	John
	4:35	ing" him. At length, having dismissed the multitude, he entered the boat, and with the Twelve, started to the other side of the sea. Being weary, Jesus soon fell asleep. A storm arose very suddenly and greatly terrified the disciples. They awoke him, and at his word, "Peace, be still," the storm ceased. The disciples wondered very greatly at the fact that "even the wind and the sea obey him" (Mark).	8:22	
to		They landed, probably early in the morning, at a village named Gergesa (now Kersa), situated close to the shore, and near which the mountain, with a rapid descent, comes close to the water's edge. Here he was met by two demoniacs "coming forth out of the tombs, exceeding fierce, so that no man could pass by that way" (Matthew). At the request of the evil spirits they were permitted, after leaving the men, to enter into a herd of swine feeding near by. The result was that the swine ran down the hillside into the sea and perished. Angered at the loss of the swine, rather than pleased at the healing of the demoniacs, the Gergesenes at once besought Jesus to depart out of their coasts. Having commissioned one of the healed demoniacs to return to his home and tell how great things the Lord had done for him, Jesus and the Twelve again entered the boat and sailed for the other	to	
	to			
9:1.	5:21.	side, where he was gladly received.	8:40.	
9:10	2:15	Upon his return to Capernaum he was immediately met by a great multitude of people. While here he accepted an invitation to a feast prepared by Levi, the former publican. During the feast he was assailed by the scribes and Pharisees for eating with publicans and sinners. He replied that his mission was	5:29	
to	to			

Matt.	Mark.		Luke.	John.

not to the good, but to the bad; not to the righteous, but to sinners. The disciples of John, some of whom were present, wanted an explanation of the feasting of his disciples as contrasted with the fasting of the disciples of John. The answer given reveals the first shadow of the cross.

9:17. *2:22.* — *to* — *5:34.*

9:18 *5:22* — *8:41*

While the feast was progressing, Jairus, a ruler of the synagogue, entered and asked that Jesus would come and heal his daughter, who was then dying. Jesus started to go with him. On the way a woman, afflicted grievously for twelve years, pressed her way through the crowd, anxious that she might have opportunity if it were but to touch the hem of his garment. She touched him, and was at once healed. Jesus, noticing that "virtue had gone out of him," turned and commended her for her faith. While he spoke with her, word was brought that Jairus's daughter was already dead; but he proceeded to the house, assuring her father that all would be well. At the house, he took with him Peter, James, and John, with the father and mother, and in their presence raised the young woman to life. This miracle, as might be expected, excited the amazement of all far and near.

to *to* — *to*

9:26. *5:43.* — *8:56.*

9:27

On the way homeward he was followed by two blind men, who went into the house after him, crying, "Have mercy on us, thou son of David" (Matthew). After asking them whether they believed him able to heal them, and receiving an affirmative reply, he touched their eyes and healed them. As these departed "there was brought to him a dumb man possessed with a devil" (Matthew), and

to

Matt.	*Mark.*	he healed him. As the multitudes looked on in amazement they said, " It was never so seen in Israel. But the Pharisees said, By the prince of the devils casteth he out devils."	*Luke.*	*John.*
9:34.				

With these events we are brought to the close of the second year of our Lord's public life, and find him all the while growing in favor with the masses of the people, but, as well, ever exciting the Pharisees to a higher pitch of enmity.

THE THIRD PUBLIC YEAR. A.D. 29.

Matt.	Mark.	*January-March.*	Luke.	John.
13:53-58	6:1	SHORTLY after the opening of the third year of his ministry, Jesus went again to Nazareth, accompanied by his disciples. On the Sabbath day he entered the synagogue and began to teach. But the people, contrasting his claim to be the Messiah with the facts of his humble origin, began to find fault, and he turned away and left them.[1] After leaving Nazareth he went again through the surrounding villages teaching. During this journey he sent out the Twelve to heal and to preach. Meanwhile Jesus continued his own work.		
9:35	*to*			
to			9:1-6.	
10:42.	6:13.			

		April.		
14:1	6:14	About this time, on Herod's birthday, occurred the beheading of John the Baptist in answer to the request of the vicious Herodias. The news of the sad occurrence was brought to Jesus by the disciples of John. Shortly afterward the Twelve returned to Jesus at Capernaum. For some time now, Jesus sought a life of privacy with his disciples, rather than of public manifestation. With this in view he withdrew, after the return of the Twelve, and went to the east side of the	9:7	
				6:1

---

[1] Some writers consider this rejection identical with that recited on page 26, but, in the opinion of the author, without good reason.

Matt.	Mark.		Luke.	John.
to	to	Sea of Galilee to "rest awhile" (Mark). But he could not be hid, for the multitude, noticing his course, went on foot around the head of the sea and "outwent them"; so that when Jesus and his disciples landed not far from Bethsaida Julias, they found a multitude already gathered. Jesus spent the day in teaching them, and in the evening was moved with compassion "because they were as sheep not having a shepherd" (Mark); and he closed the day with the wonderful miracle, the feeding of five thousand men, besides women and children, with five loaves and two	to	
14:21.	6:44.	fishes. [1]	9:17.	to
14:22	6:45	After Jesus had fed the multitude they were anxious to take him by force and make him king; [2] but he sent them and the disciples away, and himself withdrew into the mountain to pray. The disciples started across the sea in the boat. During the night their progress was hindered by a storm. Toward morning Jesus came to them walking on the sea. Not knowing him at first, they were frightened, but when Jesus said, "Be of good cheer; it is I; be not afraid" (Matthew), they were so encouraged that Peter, in response to Jesus' permission, started to walk to him on the		6:21.
to	to	water. He succeeded well until he turned his eyes upon the waves, when he began to sink. In answer to his cry, "Lord, save me" (Matthew), Jesus reached forth his hand and rescued him. They entered the boat and soon reached the shore, finding themselves in the land of Gennesaret, south of Capernaum. Immediately many		

[1] This miracle occurred about the time of the Passover. It seems that Jesus did not attend this Passover.

[2] This event marks the point at which the popularity of Jesus with the common people reached its highest point. He was never popular with the rulers and Pharisees.

Matt.	Mark.		Luke.	John.
14:36.	*6:56.*			

sick people were brought to him, and he healed them; some were healed by only touching his clothes.

Meanwhile those whom he had fed the day before hurried back to Capernaum. Leaving Gennesaret, Jesus and the Twelve returned to Capernaum also, where he addressed the expectant crowd in a discourse of great beauty, but in which, greatly to the confusion of the multitude, he denominated himself "the bread of life" (John), of which man must eat in order to attain to eternal life. It made no difference that he told them afterward that the words which he spoke were "spirit" and "life." The explanation was of no avail. The Jews were offended, as were also a number of his disciples, several of whom refused to follow him any longer. As he saw them turn away, Jesus addressed the Twelve with the inquiry, "Would ye also go away?" and received from Peter the beautiful and forcible reply: "Lord, to whom shall we go? thou hast the words of eternal life. And we have believed and know that thou art the Holy One of God" (John). Following this, Jesus pointed out to them the fact that though he had chosen them all, yet one of them was a "devil."

6:22

to

6:71.

May-September.

15:1	*7:1*

About this time a company of scribes and Pharisees from Jerusalem gathered about the Saviour, and objected to his allowing his disciples to eat without first washing their hands, thus disregarding the traditions. Jesus replied to them kindly, yet with a severe rebuke to their ill-concealed hypocrisy.

Matt.	Mark.		Luke.	John.
to	to	Again desiring retirement, he left Capernaum with his disciples and withdrew to the region of Tyre and Sidon in Phœnicia.[1] His presence soon became known, and a woman of that section came to him with the request that he heal her demoniac daughter. For a while he seemed to refuse her request, saying, "It is not meet to take the children's bread and cast it to the dogs." But upon receiving her reply, "Yea, Lord: for even the dogs eat of the crumbs which fall from their master's table," he replied, "O woman, great is thy faith" (Matthew), and healed her daughter.		
15:28.	7:30.			
15:29	7:31	At length he left this region and returned through the Decapolis to a mountain on the east side of the Sea of Galilee. Here again great multitudes assembled as soon as his presence became known, bringing with them many in need of healing, and he healed them. The people were very greatly surprised as they witnessed these manifestations of power, but their surprise was still greater when, after three days' continuance with him, he fed four thousand men, besides women and children, with seven loaves and a few little fishes. He then sent the people away, and taking ship returned to the coasts of Magdala and Dalmanutha, villages on the west side of the sea, not far from Capernaum. After this he was met at Capernaum by a number of scribes and Pharisees, who demanded a confirmation of his authority by some "sign." He replied, referring them to the sign of the prophet Jonah. Again he departed by boat to the east side of the sea, and on the way warned his disciples of the		
to	to			

[1] This was his only visit to heathen territory.

Matt.	Mark.		Luke.	John.
		danger of the leaven—the teachings—of the Pharisees and Sadducees. Coming to Bethsaida Julias he was met by a blind man, who, in being healed, was able first		
16:12.	8:26.	to see men, "as trees, walking" (Mark).		
16:13	8:27	Again desiring a season of retirement, he took the Twelve and started to the region of Cæsarea Philippi. On the way he		
		inquired of the disciples, "Who do men say that the Son of man is?" Peter answered, expressing the belief of the disciples, "Thou art the Christ, the Son of the living God" (Matthew). Continuing to speak with his disciples, he surprised	9:18	
to	to	them greatly by telling them of his having to suffer a violent death, and of the certainty of his resurrection. Peter's unwillingness to hear these words led him to reply to Jesus in such a manner as to call forth from the Master a severe rebuke. After this Jesus spoke to them very plainly as to the conduct of those who would be his disciples.	to	
16:28.	9:1.	About a week later the Transfiguration		
17:1	9:2	occurred.[1] Only Peter, James, and John were permitted to witness this wonderful scene, when "His face did shine as the sun, and his garments became white as the light" (Matthew). Upon coming down from the mountain after the Transfiguration, the father of a lunatic child came to Jesus, requesting that he heal		
to	to	his child. The disciples had attempted to give relief, but found the case one beyond their control. At the word of Jesus relief was immediately realized.	9:45.	
		After the Transfiguration they crossed over the Jordan near its sources and returned through Galilee to Capernaum.		

[1] The place of the Transfiguration was probably Mount Hermon, one of the southern peaks of the Lebanon Mountains.

Matt.	Mark.		Luke.	John.
17:23.	9:32.			

On the way he spoke again concerning his death and resurrection.

Matt.	Mark.		Luke.	John.
17:24	9:33			

At Capernaum the collector of the temple tax of half a shekel came to Peter and asked whether their master was not accustomed to pay this tax. Peter replied in the affirmative. Jesus afterward inquired of Peter whether it was customary with kings to collect taxes of their own sons, or of strangers. Upon receiving from Peter the answer that they collected of strangers, and not of those of their own house, Jesus replied, "Therefore the sons are free." But lest he should give offense he sent Peter to the sea, with the direction, "Cast a hook, and take up the fish that first cometh up; and when thou hast opened his mouth thou shalt find a shekel; that take and give unto them for me and thee" (Matthew). Following this, Jesus spoke of those who are greatest in the kingdom of heaven, and illustrated his teaching by a little child. Continuing he spoke of "offences" and of "forgiveness," closing with the parables of the Lost Sheep and the Unmerciful Servant.

(Matt. *to* 18:35.) (Mark. *to* 9:50.) (Luke 9:46-50)

October-December.

About this time Jesus sent his disciples to Jerusalem to attend the feast of Tabernacles, and a few days later went up himself, "not publicly, but as it were in secret" (John).[1]

(John 7:2)

---

[1] From the point that we have now reached in the Saviour's life, until the beginning of Passion Week, the order of the events is quite uncertain, and it is exceedingly difficult to decide on an arrangement with satisfaction. This results from the following considerations: 1. Neither Matthew nor Mark gives any record of this period. 2. Luke and John, who give all the record we have, narrate but very little, if indeed anything, in common. 3. They give nothing to indicate where one supplements the other. A few things we learn quite definitely from John : (1) Jesus attended the feast of Tabernacles, October 11-18. (2) He attended the feast of Dedication, December 20-27. (3) Immediately after the feast of Dedication he withdrew to Bethabara, across the Jordan. (4) After some time he returned

Matt.	*Mark.*		*Luke.*	*John.*

At the feast of Tabernacles Jesus taught in the temple, and the Jews took offense, ostensibly because at the feast of the Passover a year and a half before, he had healed an impotent man at the pool of Bethesda on the Sabbath. But Jesus continued his teaching, and many of the people became deeply interested in his doctrine. This excited the priests and Pharisees still more, and they sent officers to arrest him. But these returned, with the reply, "Never man so spake" (John). Even more were his enemies aroused when Nicodemus, a member of the Sanhedrin, who had come to Jesus by night two and one-half years before, asked the seemingly favorable question, "Doth our law judge a man, except it first hear him for himself and know what he doeth?" This caused the enemies of Jesus to turn upon Nicodemus with the demand: "Art thou also of Galilee? Search, and see that out of Galilee ariseth no prophet" (John).

to

7:52.

to Bethany to raise Lazarus. (5) Immediately after this he withdrew to Ephraim, where he seems to have remained until time to go to the Passover. Luke narrates a number of events that seem to have occurred during this same period, none of which are named by John. The record of these events occupies the Gospel of Luke between chapters 9:51 and 13:35. In this record he mentions a journey from Galilee to Jerusalem, which was preaunounced by "the seventy," and therefore so public that it does not seem reasonable to identify it with the journey to the feast of Tabernacles named by John, which was made "in secret." These two journeys to Jerusalem necessitate an intervening return journey, although no such return is recorded. So hold Andrews, Farrar, Ebrard, Lichtenstein, Greswell, and others. This is the theory accepted by the author of this work.

But accepting this much as determined, it yet remains to arrange the events named by Luke in harmony and connection with those given by John. In doing this the position is taken that following the feast of Tabernacles Jesus returned to Galilee, of which return we have no record, and that the journey to Jerusalem recorded by Luke as occurring at this period, is the journey to the feast of the Dedication, the last journey made from Galilee to Jerusalem, and that this journey was made through Peræa, or Judæa beyond Jordan. (See Matt. 19:1; Mark 10:1; Alford on Luke 9:51; Andrews's "Life of Our Lord," pp. 366-385; Farrar's "Life of Christ," pp. 274-282.)

This journey perhaps occupied considerable time, and we are not sure that Luke narrates the events that he gives in the order of their occurrence. One event, the healing of the lepers, which he narrates much later, should, in the opinion of the author, be placed as occurring during this journey, as we have no evidence that after this Jesus "passed through the midst of Samaria and Galilee" (Luke 17:11).

Matt. *Mark* Jesus then withdrew to the Mount of *Luke.* *John.*
Olives, where he spent the night, prob-   7:53
ably in the home of Mary, Martha, and
Lazarus. Early the next morning he
returned to the temple, where occurred
the incident of the woman taken in adul-
tery.[1] After this Jesus continued his
plain and forcible teaching. He reproved
the Jews sharply for their claiming to be
the children of Abraham while they did
none of the works of Abraham, and
closed with the assertion to the Jews
so remarkable, "Before Abraham was, I
am." This claim to superiority over even
Abraham they were not slow to under-
stand; it enraged them so that they
attempted at once to stone him, as guilty
of blasphemy. Passing out from them
and out of the temple, he met a man
blind from his birth. The disciples in-   *to*
quired whether this blindness was the
result of the man's own sin or the sin
of his parents. Jesus replied that it was
not because of the sin of either, "but
that the works of God should be made
manifest in him." He then spat on the
ground and took of the moistened clay,
and with it anointed the man's eyes, and
directed him to wash in the pool of Si-
loam. The man returned from the washing in full possession of his sight. As
this also occurred on a Sabbath day, the
Pharisees again became greatly aroused,
and instituted a rigid investigation of
the case, resulting in the excommuni-
cation of the fortunate unfortunate. He
afterward met Jesus and accepted him
as the Son of God. The Saviour contin-

---

[1] This incident is omitted entirely from many of the ancient manuscripts, and is con-
sidered questionable as to its genuineness by Alford, Andrews, and others ; it is bracketed
in the Revised Version.

Matt.	Mark.		Luke.	John.

ued to teach the people, and in his address spoke the parable of the Good Shepherd.

Luke. 9:51

After the feast Jesus returned to Galilee. We next meet him "when the days were well-nigh come that he should be received up," and "he stedfastly set his face to go to Jerusalem." His intention was to go through Samaria, but as the messengers sent before him were rejected,

to

Matt. 19:12. *Mark.* 10:1.

he turned aside to cross over into Peræa. His rejection by a Samaritan village excited James and John to request the privilege of commanding fire to fall from heaven and consume them, as Elijah had once done. But Jesus rebuked the disciples, and turned aside to another village.

9:56.

During his journey eastward, on the borders of Samaria and Galilee occurred the incident of the healing of the ten lepers, only one of whom returned to give glory to God for the favor conferred, and he a Samaritan. On the way Jesus spoke to one who proposed to become his disciple, but who wished to go first and bury his father. About this time, or it may be before leaving Galilee, occurred the sending out of "the seventy." The length of time occupied in their mission is not given; the field of their activity seems to have been Peræa.

17:11-19

9:61-62.

10:1

to

Many other interesting events occurred during this final journey from Galilee. A lawyer inquired the way of life, and in replying to him Jesus gave the parable of the Good Samaritan. His disciples asked him to teach them to pray, and he taught them the Lord's Prayer, first given in the Sermon on the Mount, and added the parable of the Friend at Midnight. He healed one who was dumb and possessed of an evil spirit, and in vindicating him-

10:37.

11:1

Matt. | *Mark.* | *Luke.* | *John.*

self replied again to the charge that he wrought his miracles by the help of Beelzebub. To a woman who pronounced the mother of Jesus specially blessed, he replied that the greater blessing is to those who hear and keep the word of God. He spoke also to a great crowd in reproof of their demanding "a sign." A Pharisee requested him to dine with him, and was greatly surprised to see Jesus sit down to eat without first washing his hands, according to Jewish custom. This furnished the Saviour opportunity to speak very plainly and forcibly of their formalism and hypocrisy. A lawyer complained because his words also condemned them, and Jesus replied to him in language no less positive. Meanwhile a great multitude gathered to hear him, and he again warned his disciples against the leaven—the doctrine—of the Pharisees. One of the company requested that Jesus would direct his brothers to make a proper division of their inheritance, and Jesus, in replying, gave the parable of the Rich Fool, and urged the importance of seeking first the kingdom of God.

to

12:59.

As he journeyed on the way, some persons came to him with a report of certain Galileans whose blood Pilate had mingled with the sacrifices at the temple, and in replying to them he spoke the parable of the Barren Fig Tree. On a Sabbath, while teaching in a synagogue, he healed a woman who had been afflicted for eighteen years. The ruler of the synagogue complained of his working on the Sabbath, and Jesus replied to him, justifying his own conduct and strongly reproving the hypocrisy of the Pharisee. Continuing his teaching he spoke the parables of

13:1

to

Matt.	Mark.		Luke.	John.
		the Mustard Seed and the Leaven, and urged strongly the importance of heart service as the only true service of God. Some Pharisees came to him, warning him of the enmity of Herod and of his desire to kill Jesus, and he replied, stating his purpose to go to Jerusalem, closing with a solemn lamentation over the fate of that city.	*13:35.*	
		He arrived at Jerusalem in time for the feast of the Dedication.[1] At some time during the feast he was walking in Solomon's Porch, a long portico at the eastern side of the temple area, and the Jews asked him to declare plainly whether he was the Messiah. Jesus replied, calling attention to his works as evidence of his character and mission, and chided them for their unbelief in the presence of all that they had seen and heard. During his conversation with them he said, "I and the Father are one," and they at once took up stones to stone him. He still continued to reason with them, but they became the more enraged, and he withdrew and went across the Jordan to Bethabara, where John at first baptized. During his attendance at the feast of Dedication he seems to have visited the home of Mary, Martha, and Lazarus at Bethany.	*10:38-42*	*10:22* *to* *10:40.*

[1] This feast occurred December 20-27. (Andrews, p. 367.)

CHAPTER VI.

THREE MONTHS IN SECLUSION. A.D. 30.

Matt.	Mark.	*January–March.*	Luke.	John.
				10:40-42

JUST how long Jesus remained in Beth-abara is not known. The people, learning of his presence in their midst, came in great numbers to see and hear him. John, who mentions the withdrawal of Jesus thither, gives no record of what occurred while he remained there. The record of Luke names some events that probably occurred at this time, and as the result of which, along with the teaching of Jesus, many were led to believe.

14:1

A chief Pharisee invited Jesus to a feast at his house on the Sabbath day. Finding there a man afflicted with the dropsy Jesus healed him, and vindicated his act so strongly that the Pharisees and lawyers present could find no further ground of complaint. Taking advantage of the occasion, he spoke the parable of the Great Supper. Great multitudes gathered about him, and knowing that they had no proper conception of his service, he spoke strongly of the necessity of self-denial upon the part of those who would be his disciples.

to

Many publicans and sinners gathered about him, and he showed his regard for them by eating with them. This again aroused the scribes and Pharisees, and in answering their criticisms he spoke three parables—the Lost Sheep, the Lost Piece

Matt.	Mark		Luke.	John.

of Money, and the Prodigal Son. To the disciples he spoke the parable of the Unjust Steward; as the Pharisees were listening, he spoke to them of the sanctity of the law, and added the parable of the Rich Man and Lazarus. Addressing his disciples again, he spoke of offenses, forgiveness, and faith. The Pharisees inquired when the kingdom of God should come, and he replied, teaching them that the important thing is not knowledge of the time of its coming, but readiness for its appearance. He then added two parables—the Unjust Judge, and the Pharisee and Publican.

17:10.

17:?

to

18:14.

It was about this time that he was called to Bethany to heal Lazarus. He tarried, however, two days after the call came; during this time Lazarus died. Then, accompanied by his disciples, probably the Twelve, though others may have been with him, he returned to Bethany. The story of his meeting with the brokenhearted sisters, and of the wonderful manner in which Lazarus was restored to life, forms a most beautiful and touching part of the Gospel by John. But the enmity of the Pharisees was again aroused. A meeting of the Sanhedrin was quickly called, and Caiaphas, the high priest, argued that the life of the nation demanded the death of Jesus; he uttered a great truth, but one that was not understood by him or them. They at once put in operation plans to attain this end, but Jesus, knowing their purposes, withdrew again from them and went to Ephraim. Here he remained for some time in retirement with his disciples; we have no record of what occurred.

11:1

to

11:57.

19:3 | *10:2* |

At length the time of the Passover

48

JESUS THE NAZARENE.

Matt.	Mark.		Luke.	John.
		drew near, and Jesus started on his last journey to Jerusalem. On the way he spoke of the lawfulness of divorce. After this little children were brought to him for his blessing; and although the disciples objected to their being brought, he said, "Suffer the little children to come	18:15	
	to	unto me; forbid them not: for of such is the kingdom of God" (Mark). "And he took them in his arms, and blessed them, laying his hands upon them" (Mark). A rich young ruler, perhaps of the synagogue,[1] accosted him in relation	to	
to		to the conditions on which eternal life may be attained. Upon being taught the necessity of extreme self-denial, the young man withdrew with a sad heart, and even		
	10:31.	the disciples were led to say, in wonder, "Then who can be saved?" (Luke.) After	18:30.	
	10:32	this he spoke the parable of the Laborers in the Vineyard. To the disciples he announced the near approach of his death at the hands of his enemies, and also assured them of his resurrection. At some point in the journey the mother of James and John came to him with the request that her sons be given positions	18:31-34	
	to	of special honor in his kingdom about to be set up, as they supposed.[2] His reply informed her that they should expect lives of service and trial rather than of position and honor.		
		As he approached Jericho two blind men besought him for healing, and he	18:35	
20:34.	10:52.	answered their request; the name of one of them was Bartimeus. At Jericho he lodged in the home of one Zaccheus, a		

[1] See Alford on Luke 18:18.

[2] Geikie holds that James and John were cousins of our Lord, and that this request may have been made on the ground of relationship. (See "New Testament Hours," pp. 70, 72.)

Matt.	Mark.		Luke.	John.

chief publican. As Jesus passed by, Zac-
cheus, being of small stature, climbed up
into a sycamore tree in order that he
might see Jesus, as he was surrounded by
the multitude. Jesus, seeing him, called
him to come down, as he intended to lodge
in his house. At this the enemies of Jesus
took offense, because, as they said, "he
is gone in to lodge with a man that is
a sinner" (Luke). As he was leaving
the city the next day he spoke the parable
of the Pounds. The narrative indicates
that on this same evening, "six days
before the passover" (John), Friday,
Nisan 8, March 31,[1] he arrived at Bethany, the home of Mary, Martha, and
Lazarus. He seems to have made his home
with them during the week following.

Luke. to *19:28.*

John. *12:1.*

---

[1] Andrews, p. 422.   Farrar, p. 325.

4

Matt.	Mark.	Saturday (Sabbath), Nisan 9, April 1.	Luke.	John.
26:6	14:3	JESUS spent the day in Bethany, and was given a supper[1] at the "house of Simon the leper" (Matthew), at which Martha served, Lazarus also being present. During the feast, Mary, the sister of Lazarus and Martha, washed the feet of Jesus with her tears, and with a box of very costly ointment anointed both his head and his feet. Judas took exception to the seeming waste, but Jesus commended Mary, saying that she had come beforehand to anoint his body for burial. On this same day, toward evening, many of the Jews who had come to Jerusalem to attend the Passover came out to Bethany to see Jesus, and Lazarus, whom Jesus had recently raised to life. This growing interest in Lazarus became a source of annoyance to the rulers, because it was promoting belief in Jesus; as a consequence they turned against Lazarus and sought to take his life.		12:1
to	to			
26:13.	14:9.			
		Sunday, Nisan 10, April 2.		to
21:1	11:1	Toward evening Jesus started to go into Jerusalem. When he arrived at Bethphage he sent two of his disciples into the village to find an ass and a colt, which they were to bring for his use.	19:29	

[1] Matthew and Mark seem to place this feast several days later, but careful attention to the records will reveal the indication that they do not claim to give the exact time.

Matt.	Mark.		Luke.	John.

The beasts were brought, and seating himself on the colt, he made what is termed his triumphal entry into Jerusalem. He was preceded by a great multitude of people who, with great demonstrations of delight, welcomed him as the son of David coming in the name of the Lord. This of course aroused the Pharisees anew, and they requested Jesus to order the people to desist; but he replied, "If these shall hold their peace, the stones will cry out" (Luke). Notwithstanding all these expressions of interest, when Jesus drew near the city, presumably as he gained the first view of the temple from the summit of Olivet, he wept, and bewailed the fate of both people and city. After reaching the city he went into the temple and simply looked about on what was to be seen, and returned to Bethany.

Matt. to *21:11.*

Mark. to to *11:11.*

Luke. to *19:44.*

John. *12:19.*

Monday, Nisan 11, April 3.

In the morning Jesus returned to the city with the disciples. It seems that he had not taken breakfast, for on the way he was hungry; he may have spent the night in prayer, terminating in a fast. On the way he saw a fig tree at some distance. Although it was not the time for figs, he went to see whether it bare any, and finding none,[1] he said, "Let there be no fruit from thee henceforward for ever" (Matthew). He then proceeded to the city, and found in the temple the same desecration of God's house that he had rebuked so emphatically three years

Mark. *11:12*

Matt. *21:18,19*

Matt. *21:12*

Mark. to

Luke. *19:45*

---

[1] "The tree was *precocious* in being clothed with leaves; and if it had had on it *winter figs*, which remain on from autumn, and ripen early the next season, they would have been *ripe at this time*. But there were none—it was a *barren tree.*"—*Alford on Mark 11:13.*

Matt.	Mark.		Luke.	John.
to		before. Seeing this, he again rebuked them, and drove out those who were buying and selling offerings for sacrifice, and overturned the tables of the money brokers who were there exchanging the temple coins for those of commerce. The scribes and Pharisees were again aroused at this seemingly unwarranted assumption of authority, but were evidently held in check by the approval that he received	to	
	11:18.	from the people; even the children cried	19:48.	
21:17.	11:19.	out, "Hosanna to the son of David" (Matthew). He returned again to Bethany to spend the night.		

Tuesday, Nisan 12, April 4,

Matt.	Mark.		Luke.	John.
21:20	11:20	Was crowded with interesting events. On their way to the city in the morning, Jesus and the disciples passed again by the fig tree, and the disciples were surprised to see it withered and dying. When they spoke of it to Jesus, he used the circumstance to teach them the importance and the potency of faith.		
to		Upon his arrival at the temple the chief priests and scribes demanded his authority for what he had done, referring, no doubt, to the authoritative manner in which he had cleansed the temple the day before. He gave them no definite reply, undoubtedly intending to say by his conduct that his acts were the seal of his authority. He then spoke to them		
		in parables, uttering the Two Sons, the Wicked Husbandmen, and the Marriage of the King's Son. He was afterward questioned	20:1	
to		in relation to the payment of tribute to Cæsar, the resurrection, the chief commandment, and the Messiah, the effort being in each case to entangle him so		

Matt.	Mark.		Luke.	John.

as to find some pretext for proceeding against him. But to all of these inquiries he gave such answers that they could only marvel at the wisdom with which he spoke. "And no man after that durst ask him any question" (Mark). He then proceeded to warn his disciples against the scribes and Pharisees, pronouncing against them many and grievous woes because of their unjustifiable hypocrisy.

Matt. 23:39.

While sitting in the court of the women, Jesus looked up at the worshipers as they deposited their gifts in the treasure chests placed there for their reception. Among others there came a poor widow, whose offering did not exceed in value one-twelfth of a cent, and as she deposited it the Lord commended her as giving more than all the others,—it was all she had. Certain Greeks, Gentile "proselytes of the gate," desired to see him, but his answer indicates that he knew that the motive behind their anxiety was simply a feeling of curiosity, and hence not particularly worthy of encouragement. Jesus was now occupied with thoughts of his approaching death, and as he spoke of this, and uttered a short prayer, there came an audible voice from heaven testifying to his character and work. He continued to speak of the importance of accepting, and the danger of rejecting, the true Light. Many of the rulers were led to believe on him.

Mark 12:41. *Luke* 21:4. *John* 12:20 *to* 12:50.

Shortly after this he left the temple for the last time. As they were passing out the disciples called his attention to the splendor of the building. This caused him to speak at length of the awful fate awaiting both city and temple. At length reaching the Mount of Olives, the disci-

Matt. 24:1. *Mark* 13:1. *Luke* 21:5.

Matt.	Mark.		Luke.	John.
		ples asked a further explanation, desiring to know especially the time of these events. This led Jesus to speak in a strange, almost enigmatical strain, in which he so combined his statements respecting the destruction of Jerusalem and respecting his own second coming, that it is for us to-day quite difficult, if not impossible, to separate them. He then spoke two parables,—the Ten Virgins and the Talents,—closing with some statements		
to	to		to	
			21:36.	
26:5.	13:37.	relative to his betrayal. After this they went to Bethany and stayed all night. It	21:37	
26:14-16	14:10, 11	was probably on this evening that Judas bargained with the chief priests for his	to	
		betrayal.[1]	22:6.	

Wednesday, Nisan 13, April 5.

He seems to have spent this day in Bethany in quiet.[2]

Thursday, Nisan 14, April 6.

THE PASSOVER.

Matt.	Mark.		Luke.	John.
		This proved to be the most eventful day of all thus far; however, not much		
26:17	14:12	occurred until evening. During most of the day Jesus remained at Bethany. He sent Peter and John into the city, probably in the earlier part of the day, to	22:7	
to	to	prepare the Passover for him and the Twelve, indicating to them how they should find a suitable room. In the evening, with the remaining ten, he went	to	
26:20.	14:17.	into the city, and proceeded directly to the room where the feast was prepared.	22:14	
		At some time during the evening, it may be while they were deciding the places	22:24-30	

[1] So Alford and Andrews. Farrar and Geikie prefer Saturday after the anointing at the house of Simon.

[2] So Andrews, Geikie, Farrar, Weiseler, Ellicott.

Matt.	Mark.		Luke.	John.

they should occupy at the table, there arose among the disciples a strife as to which of them should be the greatest in the coming kingdom. Noticing this, Jesus, in order to teach them a lesson of humility, took a basin of water and proceeded to wash their feet, a service which they should have performed for him instead. After this, while eating the feast, he told them that one of them should betray him, and, to John at least, pointed out Judas as the traitor. Judas, noticing that his purposes were being made known, withdrew at once to complete the betrayal; the other disciples thought that he went out to secure something for the further days of the feast. After Judas had withdrawn, possibly before, Jesus instituted the ordinance of the Lord's Supper, and spoke of what was about to come upon him; he warned them also that during the night they would all desert him. Peter's self-assurance caused the Lord to warn him especially. He continued to speak to them, discoursing respecting the Comforter, and of the necessity of their "abiding" in him, closing the evening service with his great intercessory prayer. They then sang a hymn, and withdrew from the room.

13:1 (John)

26:21-25 (Matt.) *14:18-21* (Mark.) — *22:21-23* (Luke.)

26:26-35 (Matt.) *14:22-25* (Mark.) — *22:15-20* (Luke.) *to* (John)

22:31-38 (Luke.)

26:30. (Matt.) *14:26* (Mark.) — *17:26.* (John)

THE ARREST.

As he had done on previous evenings, Jesus started in the direction of Bethany, accompanied by the Eleven. When they arrived at the garden of Gethsemane he turned aside and entered the enclosure. Leaving eight of the number at the entrance, he took with him Peter, James, and John and withdrew into the midst of the garden, "and began to be sorrow-

22:39 (Luke.) *18:1.* (John)

26:36 (Matt.)

Matt. | *Mark.* | | *Luke.* | *John.*

ful and sore troubled" (Matthew). He then withdrew from the three and prayed for some time; when he returned he found them all asleep. Twice more did he withdraw for prayer, and each time upon his return he found the disciples asleep. Upon his return the third time, Judas appeared with a band of officers and a multitude of people who had come out to arrest him. When Jesus saw them coming he went to them and asked, "Whom seek ye?" They told him that they were seeking Jesus of Nazareth, and he replied, "I am he," and the crowd fell back in confusion. He repeated the question, and to their reply said again, "I am he" (John). Judas, seeing that they were awaiting his action, stepped forward and, according to the prearranged plan, saluted Jesus with "Hail, Rabbi; and kissed him" (Matthew). The officers then arrested Jesus. Peter, however, drew a sword brought from the room of the supper, and smote a servant of the high priest, cutting off his right ear. At once Jesus healed the wound and bade Peter put up his sword. The disciples, seeing Jesus in the hands of his enemies, took to flight, except that a young man, possibly Mark, followed him for some distance and then also fled. Peter and John, recovering at length from their fright, followed at a distance, and through the influence of John were admitted into the palace of the high priest. The arrest occurred probably about midnight.

Friday, Nisan 15, April 7.

THE TRIAL.

Jesus was taken at once to Annas, ex-high priest and father-in-law to Caiaphas,

Matt. column: *to* ... 26:56.

Mark. column: *to* ... 14:52.

Luke. column: *to* ... 22:53.

John. column: 18:2 ... *to* ... *to*

Matt.	Mark.		Luke.	John.
26:57	14:53	probably in recognition of his influence. After a very brief hearing he sent him to Caiaphas, the high priest, where the members of the Sanhedrin were already assembled, probably about 1 A.M. After repeated efforts to find testimony against him had failed, they informally pronounced him worthy of death because he had openly avowed that he was the Christ, the Son of the Blessed, and then adjourned to meet after daylight to ratify the finding. During this trial occurred the denial of Peter, while standing with the enemies of Jesus in the open court around a fire. When the Sanhedrin adjourned they left Jesus in the hands of the rabble, by whom he was greatly abused, being spit upon, blindfolded, and smitten on the face. After daybreak the Sanhedrin again assembled and, after a few questions, formally pronounced sentence against him, and immediately led him to Pilate, the Roman procurator, to have their sentence confirmed, as they had no authority to inflict the death penalty.	22:54	
to	to		22:55	18:27.
			to	
27:2.	15:1.		23:1.	
27:3		Judas, learning that Jesus was condemned and in a fair way to death, repented of his treachery and brought the money back to the chief priests, and then went out and hanged himself.		
	15:2	Jesus was now before Pilate. His accusers did not enter the judgment hall, because going into the house of a Gentile would defile them, and they would not be permitted to participate further in the feast; hence, Pilate came out to them, and demanded their charge. They first accused Jesus of being a malefactor, and Pilate at once directed them to take him and judge him themselves. But this they had no authority to do. He then	23:2	18:28
to				to
	to		to	

Matt.	Mark.		Luke.	John.

took Jesus with him into the hall of judgment and asked him, "Art thou the King of the Jews?" (Luke.) Though Jesus replied in the affirmative, Pilate turned to the Jews with the statement, "I find no fault in this man" (Luke). Still further aroused by the manifest danger that their wishes would not be gratified, they charged Jesus with creating disturbance among the people even from Galilee to Jerusalem.

(Matt. 27:11. Mark. 15:5. Luke 23:5. John 28:28.)

Hearing mention of Galilee, Pilate was pleased, because Herod, the tetrarch of Galilee, was then in the city, and he at once sent Jesus to him for trial. Herod was also pleased with this, because for a long time he had desired to see Jesus. But he was disappointed when Jesus refused to reply to any of his inquiries; he also hoped to see him work some miracle. The silence of Jesus in his presence caused Herod to turn against him, and he made Jesus an object of derision before the members of his court, and then returned him to Pilate. This compliment of Pilate to Herod resulted in the restoration of friendship between the two rulers.

(Luke 23:6 to)

Upon the return of Jesus, Pilate addressed the Jews, saying that neither he nor Herod had found any fault with Jesus, and hence he would release him according to the custom to release one prisoner during the Passover. But they vehemently objected, demanding instead the release of one Barabbas, a notorious insurrectionist and murderer. When Pilate asked what he should do with Jesus, they cried out at once, "Crucify, crucify him" (Luke). About this time Pilate's wife, Claudia Procula, sent a message to Pilate urging him to have nothing to do

(Matt. 27:15. Mark. 15:6. to to Mark. 15:14. Luke 23:21. John 18:39,40)

Matt.	Mark.		Luke.	John.
		with the case, as she had suffered much in a dream concerning Jesus. Pilate then proposed to scourge him and let him go		
	15:15-20	free. But to this his enemies would not consent. They still called for his crucifix-		*19:1*
		ion and for the release of Barabbas. Pilate yielded, and ordered Jesus to be scourged		
27:23.		preparatory to crucifixion. But yet he half repented, and renewed his efforts for the release of Jesus; but the Jews renewed their attack, now demanding his death because he claimed to be the Son of God. This accusation caused Pilate to take him again into the judgment hall. After ex- amining him further, he seemed deter- mined to release him. But now the Jews raised the cry that if he released Jesus he would show himself disloyal to Cæsar. This aroused a fear of Cæsar that quickly		
27:24		influenced Pilate's mind. He then took water and washed his hands, thus indi- cating that he was unwilling to bear any part of the responsibility in the case, and	*23:22-25*	
to		pronounced final sentence of death, and Jesus was delivered over to be crucified.		*to*
		The soldiers to whom he was delivered, taking advantage of his seemingly help- less situation, heaped upon Jesus all		
27:31.		manner of mockery and insult. When they led him out to crucifixion they laid upon him the transverse beam of the		
27:32,33	*15:21,22*	cross.[1] But this soon proved too heavy for Jesus in his exhausted condition, and they compelled one Simon of Cyrene to bear it. They were followed by many wo- men of the city, weeping because of the fate that awaited Jesus; but he told them	*23:26*	

[1] "The cross was an upright pale or beam, intersected by a transverse one at right angles. . . . To this cross the criminal, being stripped of his clothes, was fixed by nails driven through the hands and (not always, nor perhaps generally,) through the feet, sepa- rate or united. The body was not *supported* by the nails, but by a piece of wood which passed between the legs."—*Alford on Matt. 27:35.*

Matt.	Mark.		Luke.	John.

they needed to weep rather for themselves and for their children. At length they reached Golgotha, the place of crucifixion.

THE CRUCIFIXION.

The hour of the crucifixion was probably about nine o'clock in the morning. *(Luke: to — John: 19:22.)* Before crucifying him they offered Jesus a drink prepared to produce stupefaction, but he declined to take it. While they were driving the nails into his flesh he spoke the first of the seven utterances on the cross, "Father, forgive them; for they know not what they do" (Luke). After the cross was erected the soldiers sat down to divide his clothes, while the rabble indulged in wild rejoicing and wicked reviling. Two thieves were crucified with him. They, too, joined in the reviling, until one at length became convinced of the superior character of Jesus and prayed, "Jesus, remember me when thou comest in thy kingdom" (Luke). Jesus replied, "To-day shalt thou be with me in Paradise" (Luke). Looking down near the cross, he saw his mother, and near her the apostle John, and he spoke the third time, saying, "Woman, behold, thy son!" and to John, "Behold, thy mother!" (John.) Following this occurred the three hours of darkness, from 12 M. to 3 P.M., during which some still lingered near the cross. As the darkness passed away Jesus cried aloud—"My God, my God, why hast thou forsaken me?" (Matthew.) Shortly after, he spoke again, "I thirst" (John); then waiting a short time, he said, "It is finished" (John), and followed this with the seventh and last utterance, "Father, into thy hands I commend my spirit" (Luke), bowed his head, and died.

Marginal references:

- Matt. 27:34-38
- Mark 15:23.
- Mark 15:24-32
- Matt. 27:39-44
- Luke 23:43.
- John 19:23, 24
- John 19:25-27
- Matt. 27:45-47
- Mark 15:33-35
- Luke 23:44, 45
- John 19:28-30
- Matt. 27:48, 49
- Mark 15:36.
- Matt. 27:50.
- Mark 15:37.
- Luke 23:46-49

Matt.	Mark.		Luke.	John.
27:51-56	15:38-41	At this the earth quaked, the veil of the temple between the Holy and the Most Holy places was rent from top to bottom, a number of graves were opened, "and many bodies of the saints that had fallen asleep were raised; and coming forth out of the tombs after his resurrection they entered into the holy city and appeared unto many" (Matthew).		
		As it was the day before the Sabbath, the Jews requested Pilate to order the soldiers to break the legs of those who had been crucified, that their death might be hurried, so that their bodies might be removed before the Sabbath. Coming to Jesus, they found him already dead, and they passed him without breaking his legs, but thrust a spear into his side.		19:31-37
27:57-61	15:42-47	Toward evening Joseph of Arimathea, a member of the Sanhedrin and a believer in Jesus ("he had not consented to their counsel and deed"—Luke), came to Pilate to obtain permission to bury the body of Jesus. Having obtained his request, he went out with Nicodemus, also a member of the Sanhedrin, and took the body of Jesus down from the cross, and laid it in his own private sepulcher, just newly built in a garden near the place of the crucifixion. A number of women observed the burial.	23:50-56	19:38-42

Saturday, Nisan 16, April 8.

| 27:62-66 | During the Sabbath (Saturday) the body of Jesus lay in the tomb. Toward evening the chief priests and Pharisees, remembering what he had said concerning rising from the dead, came to Pilate and requested him to station a guard at the tomb, lest the disciples should come and steal the |

| *Matt.* | *Mark.* | body away. Desiring to please them, Pilate granted the request, and they placed the governor's seal on the tomb, and stationed a guard of Roman soldiers to prevent any interference on the part of the disciples. |

CHAPTER VIII.

RESURRECTION, APPEARANCES, AND ASCENSION.

Matt.	Mark.	*Sunday, Nisan 17, April 9.*	Luke.	John.
		THE RESURRECTION.		
28:1	16:1	EARLY in the morning of the first day of the week, Mary Magdalene and Mary the mother of James, and Salome, with perhaps other women, having prepared the necessary articles, started to the tomb to complete the anointing of the body of Jesus, evidently not aware of the sealing of the tomb and the placing of the guard.	24:1	20:1
		At some time in the morning there was an earthquake, and the angel of the Lord rolled back the stone from the tomb and sat upon it. At the sight of him the guards were affrighted, and fell back as		
to	to	dead men.		
		The women at length drew near, wondering as they came how the great stone should be removed from the door of the sepulcher. But when they came in sight of the tomb they saw the stone already	to	
·		removed. The guard had left before this time, and the women went on to the tomb, and at length entered it, only to be thrice surprised,—at the absence of		to
		Jesus' body, and at the presence of two apparently young men, who still further surprised them by telling them that Jesus was not there, but had risen, and that		
28:8.	16:8.	they should go and tell his disciples. Mary Magdalene hurriedly left the tomb		

Matt.	Mark.		Luke.	John.

and went into the city, where she met Peter and John. She told them what they had seen and heard, and the two, greatly excited, ran to the sepulcher, Mary following after them. John ran the faster, and reaching the tomb, stooped down, and looking in saw nothing but the burial clothes. Peter, coming shortly afterward, entered the tomb, and John followed him, and both were convinced that Jesus had risen. They then returned to the city. *24:12.*

THE APPEARANCES ON SUNDAY.

16:9-11. Mary Magdalene reached the tomb soon after John and Peter left, and stood outside weeping. Presently Jesus appeared to her, but she did not recognize him until he addressed her by name. About this same time he appeared to the other women also, with the salutation, "All hail" (Matthew). *20:18.*

28:9, 10.

16:12,13 During the day two of the disciples went to Emmaus. On the way Jesus appeared to them, but concealed his identity until in the evening during supper, when they recognized him in the breaking of bread; "and he vanished out of their sight" (Luke). Excited by this, they immediately returned to the city, where they found the Eleven met together discussing an appearance of Jesus to Peter. *24:13.*

to

16:14. They reported his appearance to them at Emmaus, and while they were talking he suddenly stood in their midst, and saluted them with "Peace be unto you" (Luke). By showing them his hands and feet he convinced them of his identity, and later he ate with them. During the evening he breathed upon them, and said, "Receive ye the Holy Ghost" (John). *20:18-23*

24:49.

| Matt. | Mark. | Monday, April 10—Wednesday, May 17. | Luke. | John. |

OTHER APPEARANCES.

Thomas was not present at the meeting on Sunday evening, and he refused to believe what the others had told him. A week later the apostles were together again, and Thomas was with them. Jesus again appeared, and asked Thomas especially to notice the evidences of his resurrection, that he might be fully convinced; and Thomas said, "My Lord and my God" (John). He did not appear again for some time, and the disciples began to return to their former occupations. On a certain occasion Peter and seven others of the apostles spent the night on the Sea of Galilee, fishing, with no success. In the early dawn they were addressed by a stranger standing on the shore, who suggested that they "cast the net on the right side of the boat" (John). They did so, and took a vast multitude of fishes. John declared at once, "It is the Lord" (John); and Peter sprang into the water and swam ashore, the others following in a boat. On the shore they found a fire kindled and some fish being cooked, preparatory to a meal. They were asked to bring of their catch and dine. After the meal, occurred that peculiarly interesting conversation between Jesus and Peter in which Peter thrice avowed his love for his Lord, whom he had recently thrice denied.

Some time after this Jesus appeared upon an unnamed mountain in Galilee, where he gave the Great Commission.[1] Paul tells us (I. Cor. 15:7) that at a later

John column: 20:24 / to / 20:29. / 21:1 / to / 21:25.
Matt: 28:16-20 Mark: 16:15-18

[1] This appearance is probably identical with that named by Paul in I. Cor. 15:6.

5

Matt. | *Mark.* | *Luke.* | *John.*

time he appeared to James, an appearance not recorded in the Gospels.

Thursday, May 18.

THE ASCENSION.

Acts.

16:19.

Forty days after his resurrection Jesus again met the disciples in Jerusalem. He there conversed with them for some time, especially reiterating the promise of the Holy Spirit, and urging them to remain in Jerusalem awaiting his coming. He then led them out near Bethany, conversing on the way. At length he lifted up his hands and blessed them, and while blessing them he was " parted from them, and was carried up into heaven " (Luke), "and a cloud received him out of their sight. And while they were looking stedfastly into heaven as he went, behold, two men stood by them in white apparel; which also said, Ye men of Galilee, why stand ye looking into heaven? this Jesus, which was received up from you into heaven, shall so come in like manner as ye beheld him going into heaven."

24:50-53   *1:4*

to

1:12.

" AMEN: COME, LORD JESUS."

APPENDIX.

Bethab'ara. A town near the river Jordan, probably east of Jericho, although it may have been farther north. It was the place where "John at first baptized," and to which Jesus retired after the feast of Dedication. Jesus was probably baptized near this place.

Beth'any. A small village situated on the eastern slope of Olivet, about one and one-half miles from Jerusalem. It was the home of Mary, Martha, and Lazarus, and was frequently visited by Jesus.

Bethes'da, Pool of. A pool located, according to Geikie, at the northwest corner of the temple area; one hundred and sixty-five feet long and forty-eight feet wide.

Beth'lehem. A village located about six miles south of Jerusalem, on a ridge 2,550 feet above sea level. Being the place of David's birth, it was called "the city of David." It was also the place of Rachel's death and burial.

Bethsa'ida. A town in Galilee, near the head of the Sea of Galilee, on the west side of the Jordan. It was the birthplace of Philip, Andrew, and Peter, and was frequently visited by Jesus. The exact location is not known.

Bethsa'ida Ju'lias. A village, afterward a city, on the east side of the Jordan, near which Jesus fed the 5,000.

Cæsare'a. The Roman capital of Judæa. It was formerly a city of great splendor, but is now inhabited only by robbers and wild animals.

Cæsare'a Philip'pi. A city situated about one hundred and twenty miles northeast of Jerusalem; perhaps visited once by Jesus.

Ca′na. The place of Jesus' first miracle; a small village, the exact location of which is not known, but probably identical with Kefr Kenna, about four miles northeast of Nazareth; some authors prefer Kâna el-Jelil, about seven miles northeast of Nazareth.

Caper′naum. An important city in the time of Jesus, but now so completely in ruin that its exact location is not known. It was near the head of the Sea of Galilee, on the west side, and was the home of Jesus during his public life.

Chora′zin. A city or village in the vicinity of Capernaum, now in ruin. The exact location is not certain.

Dalmanu′tha. A town south of Capernaum on the seashore. The exact location is not known.

Dead Sea. The size of this sea is about ten by forty-six miles. The surface is 1,300 feet below sea level. The water is clear and beautiful, but salt and bitter. The sea contains no living thing, and has no outlet. The cliffs on the west side are 1,500 to 2,200 feet high.

Decap′olis. A district of country east of the Jordan, and extending from a short distance south of the Sea of Galilee north as far as Damascus, including ten cities. The boundaries are not definitely determined.

Dedication, Feast of. An annual feast of rejoicing, kept in commemoration of the renewal of the temple service after its suspension by Antiochus Epiphanes, B.C. 167. It continued one week.

Em′maus. A small village probably seven or eight miles northeast of Jerusalem. The exact location is uncertain.

E′phraim. A town or city about eight miles north of Jerusalem. The exact location is uncertain.

Gal′ilee, Sea of. Its size is eight by fifteen miles, and its surface is six hundred and eighty-two feet below sea level. The course of the Jordan is perceptible throughout the entire length of the sea. On account of the depression of the sea below the surrounding country, it is subject to very sudden storms, especially from the winds coming over the eastern tablelands. It is very full of fish.

Genues'aret. A plain on the west shore of the Sea of Galilee, south of Capernaum, about one mile wide and three miles long. It was very productive.

Gethsem'ane. An olive garden or orchard on the west slope of Olivet. Its exact location is somewhat disputed.

Gol'gotha. The place of the crucifixion. By tradition, it is held to be near the site of the Church of the Holy Sepulcher, on the west side of, and within, the present city of Jerusalem. Modern investigators, however, quite generally prefer a point just north of the city. It was near, yet without, the city in the time of Christ.

Hat'tin, Horns of. A row of hills or low mountains on the west side of the Sea of Galilee, not far from Capernaum; probably the place of the Sermon on the Mount.

Her'mon, Mount. The most conspicuous mountain in Palestine. It is one of the peaks at the southern extremity of the Anti-Lebanon range. Its height is 10,000 feet. It was probably the scene of the Transfiguration.

Herods of the New Testament. Herod was the name of an Indumæan family who, under Roman authority, ruled over the Jewish nation in New Testament times. The name is applied to four different persons by New Testament writers.

1. *Herod the Great*, called, in Matthew 3 : 1, "Herod the king." He was a son of Antipater, who was made procurator of Judæa by Julius Cæsar B.C. 47. Antipater made his son, Herod the Great, governor of Galilee. B.C. 40 he was made king of Judæa by act of the Roman senate. He slew his wife's grandfather Hyrcanus, Mariamne his favorite wife, and three of his sons, Alexander, Aristobulus, and Antipater. He died B.C. 4.

2. *Herod Antipas*, called "the tetrarch," and twice "the king" (Matt. 14 : 9; Mark 6 : 4). He was the son of Herod the Great, brother of Archelaus, half-brother of Philip I., whose wife he incestuously married, and also half-brother of Philip II., tetrarch of the Bashan district. He was appointed tetrarch of Galilee after the death of his father, Herod the Great, and ruled till A.D. 38. He slew John the Baptist. Jesus appeared before him in his trial.

3. *Herod Agrippa I.* was the son of Aristobulus (mentioned under No. 1) and grandson of Herod the Great. He was made governor of the Bashan district by the emperor Caius Caligula A.D. 37; later was given Peræa and Galilee, and in A.D. 41 was given also Judæa and Samaria, thus possessing a territory equal to that of Herod the Great. It was by his order that the apostle James was slain and Peter thrown into prison. He died suddenly and very miserably at Cæsarea, A.D. 44. See Acts 12 : 21-23.

4. *Herod Agrippa II.* He was the son of Agrippa I., and was given the principality of Chalcis by the emperor Claudius A.D. 48. Four years later he was given instead the former tetrarchies of Philip II. and Lysanias, with the title of king, and in connection with this the superintendence of the temple at Jerusalem. In A.D. 55 the emperor Nero added to his dominions several cities and villages of Galilee. It was before him that Paul made the address of Acts 26. He died at Rome A.D. 100, in his seventieth year.

Jer'icho. The first city conquered by Joshua; fifteen miles from Jesusalem, a little north of east; about six miles west of the Jordan.

Jeru'salem. The most important city of Palestine. The elevation above sea level is 2,500 feet. It is built on two summits—Mt. Moriah and Mt. Zion. The Tyropœan Valley divides the city from north to south; the valley of Kedron or Jehoshaphat passes on the east side, and the valley of Hinnom on the west and south sides. *History.*— Probably Salem of Genesis 14:18; captured by David, B.C. 1046; by Shishak of Egypt, B.C. 970; recaptured by Jehoash, king of Israel, B.C. 830; fortified by Uzziah, B.C. 807; improved by Jonathan and Hezekiah, B.C. 755 to 726; city and temple pillaged by Egyptians, B.C. 609; captured by Nebuchadnezzar, B.C. 606 to 598; temple repaired by order of Cyrus king of Persia, B.C. 536 to 516; Ezra made governor, B.C. 469; captured by Alexander the Great, B.C. 322; captured and plundered by Ptolemy, of Egypt, B.C. 324; captured by Antiochus the Great, B.C. 200; temple profaned by Antiochus Ephiphanes, B.C. 167; the Maccabees obtained control B.C. 163; invaded and captured by Lysias, the governor of Syria, about B.C. 160; recaptured by Simon Maccabeus, B.C. 142; captured by Pompey of Rome, B.C. 63;

city and temple destroyed by Titus of Rome, A.D. 70; rebuilt by Hadrian, A.D. 131; Barcocheba, a Jew, obtained possession A.D. 132; recaptured by Romans, A.D. 135, and named Ælia Capitolina. The Jews were not allowed afterward to enter the city until the middle of the fourth century. Pilgrimages of Christians to Jerusalem began A.D. 326, when it was visited by Helena, the mother of Constantine. Since the fall of the Roman empire, the city has many times been captured and recaptured. It has been in the hands of the Turks since A.D. 1847.

Jor'dan River. The principal river of Palestine, and the only river named in the Gospels. Its sources are in the Lebanon Mountains, and it empties into the Dead Sea. In its course it falls 3,012 feet. It is narrow, deep, and swift till near its mouth. It is very crooked, its length, following its course between the Sea of Galilee and the Dead Sea, being more than three times its direct length.

Judæ'a, Wilderness of. A district of country extending from Bethany to the Jordan and south, mountainous and waste, and never cultivated, being occupied chiefly by robbers.

Machærus. A strong fortress on the frontier of Peræa and Arabia. Josephus says that it was the place of the execution of John the Baptist,[1] and hence was probably the place of his imprisonment.

Mag'dala. A town on the west shore of the Sea of Galilee, south of Capernaum. Its exact location is not known.

Mori'ah, Mount. The summit on which the temple stood. Its height is about 2,500 feet.

Na'in. A small town of Galilee, situated about four miles from Mt. Tabor and twenty-five miles southwest of Capernaum.

Naz'areth. The home of Jesus during his early life. It is situated among the mountains, 1,200 feet above sea level, twenty-five miles from Capernaum, and about sixty miles from Jerusalem. It was unknown to history previous to New Testament times. Its present population is about 4,700.

---

[1] Antiquities, XVIII., 5, 2.

Olives, Mount of. A rounded hill east of Jerusalem, and separated from the city by the valley of Kedron. Its summit is about one-fifth of a mile from the temple on an air line; by the road, 3,075 feet. Its height is 2,700 feet.

Pal'estine. *Names.*—Canaan, Holy Land, Palestine. *Size.*—About one hundred and ninety-three miles long by seventy-five miles average width. *Divisions in Time of Christ.*—Judæa, Samaria, and Galilee west of the Jordan; Peræa and Philip's tetrarchy east. Generally mountainous. *Climate.*—Very fine in the dry season; slight frosts in winter. *Products.*—Wheat, barley, millet, fruits. *History.*—Palestine was settled by descendants of Canaan, the fourth son of Ham, and was for ages the home of idolatrous tribes. It was conquered by Joshua, B.C. 1451 to 1425, and remained in possession of Israel until B.C. 721, when the northern part was conquered by Sargon, king of Assyria. B.C. 586 the southern part was conquered by Nebuchadnezzar, and in B.C. 536 the entire country became subject to Cyrus, king of Persia, who permitted the return of the Jews carried captive to Babylon, and the rebuilding of the temple destroyed by Nebuchadnezzar. B.C. 332 the country was conquered by Alexander the Great, and in B.C. 312 it passed under the control of the Seleucidæ, between whom and the Ptolemies of Egypt it alternated until B.C. 198, when the power of the Ptolemies was broken, and Palestine was again subject to the Seleucidæ. Thus it remained until B.C. 158, when the Jews, under the leadership of the Macca-bees, again secured national independence. This condition continued till the conquest by Rome, B.C. 63. The Jews again rebelled against the Roman authority in A.D. 66, and were reconquered by Titus A.D. 70. In the sixth century the country was conquered by the Mohammedans, and in A.D. 1099 was recaptured by the Crusaders and again placed under European rule. In A.D. 1187 it was again conquered by the Mohammedans, and in A.D. 1517 by the Turks, who, notwithstanding several subsequent defeats, still hold posses-sion.

Pass'over. The greatest of the Jewish feasts, and one of the three which all of the Jews were required to attend, if possible. It was kept in memory of the deliverance from Egypt. It began with the feast of unleavened bread, which was eaten on the evening of the close of the 14th Nisan, counting the day to end at sunset. It continued for one week. Josephus says that frequently 3,000,000 people attended the feast, and that as many as 256,000 lambs were slain and eaten. On account of their system of keeping time, using intercalary months, the feast did not occur each year at the same time in the year. In the year of the crucifixion, Nisan 14 fell on April 6, counting that Nisan 14 closed at sunset.

Pen'tecost. The second of three great annual feasts. It occurred fifty days after the Passover, and lasted but one day. It was the Jewish harvest-home.

Phar'isees. The extreme religionists of the Jews in the time of Christ, especially devoted to the observance of the law as interpreted by the traditions. They were ritualists rather than moralists. They formed the middle class of people, were more numerous than the Sadducees, and were bitter enemies of Jesus.

Publicans. This name represents neither a class nor a party, but rather an occupation. They were men who followed buying of the government the privilege of collecting the taxes in certain districts, which implied the right to exact of the people about as they chose. They were especially noted for oppression and extortion. They were greatly hated by the Jews, and were classed among the very lowest.

Pu'rim. An annual feast in the month of March, kept in memory of the deliverance of the Jews from the murderous intentions of Haman.

Rabbis. These were teachers. The term is almost, but not entirely, synonymous with *scribe*. The recognized rabbis in the time of Christ were chiefly Pharisees. Their teaching was held to be superior in authority to that of the law. The Mishna declares it a greater crime to speak against the rabbis than against the law.

Sad'ducees. In the time of Christ, the liberalists, in teaching and practice. They discredited traditions, and accepted only the teaching of Moses. They were moralists rather than ritualists, and constituted the more wealthy class of the community—the upper classes. They were a comparatively small party, and were unpopular with the masses. They denied the immortality of the soul and the resurrection.

Scribes. Copyists and teachers of the law. They were mostly Pharisees, but were not confined to any party.

Si'don. One of the oldest cities of the world,—the "mother of Phœnicia,"—situated on the east coast of the Mediterranean.

Sil'oam, Pool of. A pool at the union of the Tyropœan and Kedron valleys, supplied with water brought in a subterranean channel from the Fountain of the Virgin, on the west side of the valley of Jehoshaphat.

Sy'char. A village of Samaria, in the valley between Mounts Ebal and Gerizim, near Jacob's well.

Synagogue. A congregation of ten or more Jews. It grew out of necessities caused by the Babylonian captivity, and assumed especial importance about the time of the Maccabees. In Jerusalem, in the time of Christ, there were four hundred and eighty synagogues. The term *synagogue* was applied to both the congregation and the place of worship.

Tabernacles, Feast of. The third of the three great annual feasts. It was kept in commemoration of dwelling in tents in the wilderness, and was a feast of thanksgiving. It began on Tisri 15, and lasted one week, the first and last days being counted Sabbaths. The last day was "the great day of the feast."

Tab'or, Mount. An isolated peak in Galilee. Its height is about 2,000 feet. By some it is thought to be the scene of the Transfiguration.

Temple, The. The temple of Christ's time was begun by Herod the Great, B.C. 20-17, but was not completed until A.D. 65. It was modeled after the temple built by Solomon. The size of the temple proper was thirty by ninety feet. It was surrounded by chambers and porticoes. It stood in a walled enclosure, the dimensions of which were about nine hundred and ninety feet on the north, one thousand feet on the east, nine hundred and ten on the south, and one thousand and sixty on the west. The outer part of this area was called the court of the Gentiles. Within this was the sacred enclosure—three hundred feet north and south by six hundred and thirty feet east and west—within which only Jews might enter. The eastern part of this enclosure was the court of the women, or "the treasury," an open space of about two hundred and forty feet square. At the east side of this space is believed to have been the portico called "Solomon's Porch," entered through the "beautiful gate." West of the court of the women was the court of Israel, an open corridor three hundred and twenty feet east and west by two hundred and forty feet north and south, sixteen feet deep on the north and south sides, and twenty-four feet on the east and west sides. Within this was the court of the priests, about two hundred and seventy-five feet long east and west by two hundred feet north and south. Within this was the temple proper—not far from the west wall of the temple area and facing east. The temple proper was divided into two parts—the Holy Place and Most Holy Place. These were separated by a heavy curtain or veil. The entire enclosure was frequently called "the temple."

Tyre. One of the most important commercial cities of antiquity, belonging to Phœnicia, on the east coast of the Mediterranean.

GENERAL INDEX.

SCRIPTURE INDEX.

MATTHEW.

79

LUKE—CONTINUED.

JOHN.

ACTS.

www.ingramcontent.com/pod-product-compliance
Lightning Source LLC
Chambersburg PA
CBHW020314090426
42735CB00009B/1342